I Don't Care What Mom Says,
"Life Sucks"

I Don't Care What Mom Says, "Life Sucks"

Craig Alan Brand

abbott press®

A DIVISION OF WRITER'S DIGEST

Abbott Press books may be ordered through booksellers or by contacting:

Abbott Press
1663 Liberty Drive
Bloomington, IN 47403
www.abbottpress.com
Phone: 1-866-697-5310

ISBN: 978-1-4582-1023-4 (sc)
ISBN: 978-1-4582-1025-8 (hc)
ISBN: 978-1-4582-1024-1 (e)

Library of Congress Control Number: 2013911308

Printed in the United States of America.

Abbott Press rev. date: 07/23/2013

To my immediate family. Without my family and their support, understanding, and strength, I would probably have been involuntarily committed, at a minimum, as a result of the ass-whopping Life has given me.

To my wife, my queen and my best friend. Thank you for the continued support, inspiration, communication, and inner strength.

To my children, whom I love and live for and who gave me the motivation to continue so as to be a positive influence in their lives and help them on their journeys. I earnestly hope that this book will teach you not to fight through Life as I have but to enjoy the travels. Life truly responds better to kindness and understanding than to a sharp tongue and fists of fury. Although Life will certainly tempt you to throw punches and use strong words, it is my hope that you will not find yourself in that position; and if you do, I hope your strength of character will enable you to suppress your iron fists. Unlike me, who fought with brawn, be smart and fight, only if you have to, with your brains. We now live in times where the pen is truly mightier than the sword, but if used correctly, the pen can work as a passable stabbing instrument!

When I am in a drunken mood, I gamble, fight, and drink. When I am in a sober mood, I worry, work, and think. When my moods are over and it's time for me to pass, I'll regret not telling each of you to come and kiss my ass.

Craig A. Brand

Life is not always roses and dreams. Life is about living. Living is a tough road traveled for which we shall shed many tears.

Craig A. Brand

TABLE OF CONTENTS

PROLOGUE

If you bought this book thinking you would read a series of humorous vignettes, guess again. This book is about Life, real life, not those fairy tales our mothers share with us as we grow up. Moms are smart and want what is best for their children. Moms want their children to grow up positive and happy, and they tell us things that they think we want to hear. If possible, moms would shield their children from the world. Moms think it best to fill our youthful heads with Disney World fictions, as Life will undoubtedly bring Cruella de Vil to our front doors. Mommy wants her children happy and visited by Mickey Mouse, not those caped in evil. However, boys and girls, Mickey Mouse only lives in Disney, and we must be prepared for the Big Bad Wolf and all of his huffing and puffing. Hopefully after reading this you will fortify your house with brick.

This is not a book about negativity, but about reality. It does not escape me how today's "reality" and perspective have changed from only a short time ago and come in so many respective shapes and sizes. However, there is a common element to any reality; everyone's version of reality is wrought with difficulties. This book was written by "little old me" (sometimes with the aid of my antidepressants). Yes, it was little old me, an average "Jack" (as "Joe" has already been taken by the plumbing trade and the 2008 US presidential campaign) with average means . . . and only an average amount of tolerance, wearing rapidly.

I hope you can understand and appreciate my unique perspective on Life. If you disagree, write your own book or count your blessings for you are one of the lucky few who has somehow escaped Life's trials and tribulations or who is just too "dazed and confused" to understand the gravity of reality. Ignorance is truly bliss, and in stressful times, so is liquor or loose drugs, which can now be purchased in Colorado! (That part is a joke, and what's life if we can't laugh a little!)

Life and those within our lives, for the most part, have been disappointments. We too are probably viewed as disappointments by the very people we consider disappointments. How ironic; but then, that's life. It starts with the taste of breast milk and small boobies. Just look at the love of your life who you just married—the girl of your dreams, your soul mate, who you would have taken a bullet for. Your spouse did what?! On your honeymoon! With your best friend! And your brother knew all about it. Hey, that's Life.

I used to say, "What did I do in a prior life that I now have to confront so much shit?" I spent a long time asking and looking, but I am now satisfied that this question plagues not just me, but everyone. The answer is, "You were born into a world controlled by a sadistic puppet master called Life." Life is not true, fair, nice, just, equitable, or caring. Life has created a game in which we are all pawns. Our individual, temporary situations depend upon where we land on the game board. Our temporary game board position can be good, bad, indifferent, happy, or sad. The amount of time you spend on that game board space depends on how quickly all the players ahead of you roll the dice and move onto their next space. Rest assured your current position will change, as will your circumstances. We only have some control of our lives while we are upon each space, but we have no control over Life itself. We cannot control the numbers thrown by the dice; nor can we control which space we will move to. You didn't do anything horrible in your past life to cause your present situation; you just landed on a space within the game board, which will change, and so too will your situation.

Chapter 1

THE GAME CALLED "LIFE"

You have heard of the game called Life. Well, where do you think the Milton Bradley Company got the idea from? We all exist within a game called "Life." Within this existence, we are but pawns on a game board, much like those used in games such as Jumanji or Monopoly. For all our ego, all our ambition and desire, and all our intelligence, our existence is linked to matters we cannot control or understand.

To what our existence is directly linked is an oft pondered question. A God? A force? A reckoning? Some type of ordained destiny? When I was younger and a lot more egotistical, I would have told you that it was I who controlled my destiny and my life. Age, experience, humility, and wisdom have taught me differently. It appears that a *game master* who is more powerful than us, and yes, even more than myself, is pulling our strings.

I believe this game master is *Life* itself. I shall be referring to *Life* as a proper noun. What exactly "Life" is will forever be the mystery left to our own beliefs, opinions, experiences, or religions. *Living* is a verb, which characterizes what we do while playing Life's game. Life is the game master controlling our living.

Chapter 2

RULES OF LIFE'S GAME: THE PLAYING BOARD

We are all born onto the playing board that is our world. We move about this board by the roll of *destined* or *ordained* dice. Each new move changes our lives for better or worse and all points in between. The faster Life moves us along, the faster the game will proceed, and thus, your turn will come again.

The "Game Board's Space Card"

After each of us rolls the ordained dice moving us to the next location, Life will deal you a *game card*. Game cards provide the instructions or boundaries for what will happen to you while you're on the space where you just landed. Cards are facedown so that no one can see what is coming until Life deals the next card. Life is the ordained card dealer for the Game Called Life.

Some people are simply dealt better cards than others. Have no fear, as the laws of physics still apply to the universe. To use a metaphorical gambler's code, since we are bringing up cards, "the cards will eventually always return to the favor of the house. You must be smart enough to know when to fold." In other words, hang on—persevere, as today's hell may be tomorrow's heaven.

Dress Code

This game requires no specific dress code. Life is hard enough, so dress to make yourself happy. In fact, Life can be deceptive, as experience will teach you never to judge a book by its cover. Camouflage is part of the survival tactics used by both the good and bad forces traveling around the same game board. Camouflage is a necessary skill set. Camouflage may deceive, misdirect, or provide false facts, or it may be a means of blending in. *Be seen without being noticed.*

Don't assume anything about anyone or anything. I remember a time when I was late for an evening flight from Costa Rica to Miami and did not have time to shower, shave, or change my clothes from my daily ranching activities. Yes, I'm a bit of a cowboy. My wife said that I wasn't offensively smelly and looked somewhat presentable, even though I was in blue jeans, boots, and a regular button-down shirt. In fairness, my jeans were ripped, but I bought them that way. After all they were Lucky Brand jeans, and I paid good money for those designer tears.

I got to the airplane gate in an absolute mess, as I'd had to run from the ticket counter and go through the hassles of security just to get to the gate minutes before my flight was to begin boarding. At the gate, two lines had already formed—a first-class line and one for the rest of the plane. I pushed my way to the front of the first-class line, as I already had my usual seat assignment, 1A. I took this flight on a regular basis and had lots of frequent flyer miles to utilize. Two well-dressed, older couples, who were traveling together, stood beside me in this line.

I was trying to tuck myself in a bit when one of the women said in broken English, "You are in the wrong line. This is for first-class passengers only."

I politely said, "Thank you for the information," and turned away from them thinking, *How rude.*

The foursome began bad-mouthing me in Spanish, not realizing that I understood. I just laughed to myself and acknowledged the ignorance and arrogance. People just aren't happy unless they can make themselves feel as if they are somehow better than the rest of us.

A moment later, the ticket crew personnel, with whom I had come to know, welcomed me and allowed me to board first. Imagine the look of surprise on the faces of these two couples when, not only was I the first person on the plane, but sitting in front of them. I had already been given a whiskey before their surprised expressions wore off. Once they did, I began speaking to these four in my broken Spanish, which added a new element of not only surprise but panic, as they immediately realized I'd understood what they had been saying about me earlier. Don't judge a book by its cover.

The Length of the Game

As we are all born on the game board, death is the only way we can finish. The "good" die young. This is an intended reward. The bad will and should live a long and unprosperous life. It's not up for you to decide who is "good" or "bad". You will simple recognize the "bad" as they are the old and unprosperous individuals you encounter while walking through Life.

The Game Board

The game board is fraught with challenges. Life has made the game incredibly exciting—mixed with a steady supply of drama, trauma, anxiety, action, comedy, thrills, and horror. You will be required to face all such challenges. For you, the game is about your actions and reactions.

A hint: You will suffer less in the game when you realize that these challenges will always be looking to knock you down. Look to persevere and get back up. Keep moving forward and handle the knockdowns by relying on the lessons you've learned from previous experience. You will suffer if you want to quit and give up. Feeling sorry for yourself will not make the experience easier or better. Know that everyone gets thrown from the horse. Get up, Cowboy, and if you can, don't forget your camouflage. You must ride to a new day's sun. Life will not allow you to stop. Life feeds on your sorrow, pity, misery, anguish, despair, and desperation. Keep moving forward and learn to duck and weave so as not to get knocked down the same way twice. In any event you must move forward; what other choice to you really have?

Foreplay

If I can use a *Star Wars* analogy, Life has placed the Dark Side of the Force within the game. I just realized that due to some unconscious and unintended writing, I managed to bet *Cowboys and Aliens* into this book within the first ten pages. These *dark forces* are present for Life's self-amusement.

During the game, you will encounter times of wonderfulness, happiness, and fulfillment. Other times may contain instances such as violence, hardships, and ruthfulness. Remember that living is not about what you encounter but about how you deal with, handle, and learn from the experience. Be a good boy or girl, and Life will release you early from the game board.

Pretext of the Game

The pretext of Life's game is nothing more than the reality in which we live. Remember that it was *not Life, but Mommy,* who told you that living was something wonderful. I'm sure that Life laughs every time it hears Mommy's rhetoric and words of comfort.

Life always takes away what we care about the most. Our most precious treasures become our greatest weaknesses. This applies to people, places, or things. Our weaknesses become tools used against us by those who want to hurt us. Protect what you want to keep. If you want to keep what is worthy of your protection, do not let others know of its existence or of its value to you. Again, camouflage. Experience has taught me to love and want less, so that Life has less to take. Living is hard; protecting what you have is more difficult.

As Life's game cards create change, so too must we accept change as part of living. So as to avoid extremes and mitigate times of famine, learn to save in times of feast. Kids, just because you have money in your wallet does not mean that you are to spend it. In fact, impress me by doing the opposite and save it.

The same physics governing the luck of the cards also mandate change. Change is inevitable and relevant to our daily game board positioning, whether within the stock market, the real estate market, our business, our grades, our happiness, our sadness, our weight, our hair, our looks, our family, our health, our being, our personal lives. Depending upon your board position, change will affect your mood, views, opinions, and judgments. While Life does draw your game card, it does not control how you live your life. Your character, your judgment, your morals, and your intelligence are independent of Life's direct control. Play smart, be smart, and use good judgment. Since you will not know what space on the game board you will be moved to, good judgment shall require you to try to think of everything and every possibility and utilize reasonable foreseeability. It is so important to think things through, to analyze actions or inactions, and to ask yourself what the consequences of your actions will be. We all hope that our better judgment will stop us from doing wrong in the first place.

Chapter 3

⤦ ⟿⟾ ⟾

THE PRICE OF LIVING

You are free to dream about roses of grandeur, blue princes, beautiful princesses, and happily ever afters. I just want to caution you that beautiful dreams can also be substituted with nightmares, dark knights, ogres, mongers, and fire-breathing dragons. I'll settle for a happy hobbit.

It is wise to always behave in the best light toward other people, especially those less fortunate. Today, you may be on top of the world, filled with arrogance, ego, and selfishness; tomorrow may be your day to fall. I am sure that you have heard the expression, "The ass that you *kicked* today may turn out to be the ass you need to *kiss* tomorrow." The traveled road of an *asshole* will always be a crappy one. But hey, without *assholes*, the rest of you *shits* wouldn't be here!

Beware of Lifestyles

Living a millionaire's lifestyle means living with a millionaire's overhead. Do not be envious of those who appear to have the glamour and glitz, as you do not have their burden of supporting and maintaining such a lifestyle. If you are having difficulty supporting your lifestyle of less, remember that supporting more is even harder. My Ford may not go as fast as your Porsche, but the monthly payments are sure easier to obtain and maintain, as it is easier to borrow or earn $300 than $1,300.

People should not be jealous or envious of the wealthy or anyone else for that matter. We each live within our own world and need to find comfort there. People should be thankful they do not have the burden of another person's overhead, responsibilities, and troubles. I'm a true believer in capitalism and rewarding those who took the risk or created the business or design. Good for them. People who do not take the risk do not deserve the right to complain about what they do not have. Don't look to other people's rewards, unless you are happy for them. Do not look to minimize the chances they took or the brainpower they used in order to achieve their reward. Good for them; be happy for them. Without rewards, no one would take risks. Don't put your hands into other people's pockets. If you want what they have, work for it, work honestly for it and hard. For if not, you will get into trouble, need the aid of a great lawyer, such as myself, and pay the lawyer any and all monies you may have received, plus a lot more.

The concept of having the wealthy pay more is a fool's notion. If you put your hands into the pockets of the wealthy, they will make up for it in other ways, such as putting less into yours. Wealth is created only if the economy allows money to spread. If those with any liquidity do not spread it around, then it never transfers to become yours. The Obama School of Economics is flawed from A-Z, and those believing in it should not bet their likelihoods.

Children need to learn finance and the reality of their family's finances. Children, listen to me, do not push your parents or yourself into taking on more overhead and debt. Your parents love you and may not be able to say "no" to you, but you should no better yourselves. Having less is truly having more. Less finances—less to worry about, less to lose, less to maintain—makes a healthier family structure. Living within your means and that of your family, brings stability and peace of mind. Translation: *happiness*. Trying to keep up with the Jones or living outside your means will only drive you crazy and make you miserable. Again, don't worry if someone else has more than you, materially. Just learn to borrow it, or use it with them. They then paid for it, bare the liability of it, and you get to enjoy it.

Most of us, for some reason, always feel we need more—more of everything. This tells you just how powerful Life has made our convictions for greed. We constantly want. We are not happy with what we have. We don't even unwrap what we have; it doesn't matter as long as we have it and then want again and more. The consequences of our actions do not matter as long as whatever we desire is ours. Greed, compulsion, and overconsumption are horrible culprits and lead to self-destruction.

Our eyes and desires are always greater than our needs. Sleep on every decision of importance or act of compulsion. Try not to spontaneously purchase, sign, act upon, take, or consume. Ask yourself if you really need what your eyes want. If you don't really need what your eyes are asking for, or if you are just appeasing your spoiled eyes, then save the money, save the resources, save the time, save your energy, and save the headache. If it is meant to be, whatever you want will always be there tomorrow or thereafter. If you are being rushed into making a decision, ask the reason for the urgency and then question your answer. Hasty decisions yield bad results. Can you afford the cost, the expense, or the risk of loss?

In business, do not go for "home runs" or business deals where you are to believe in fame and fortune. Every batter from time to time will hit a home run if he or she keeps swinging. The key to making the deal become a reality is to run the bases one at a time and keep swinging, as eventually you will connect. Striking out is part of the game and should be expected. Don't lose faith, don't get frustrated, and don't feel like a loser for striking out. Concentrate, better yourself, and be smart, and you will connect with the ball. Striking out allows your skin to thicken and your experience and resources to grow and develop. However, it will be those little singles and doubles that you hit that will keep bread on your table and your bills paid.

Maturity and experience teach us not to waste time and resources on personal collections. Personal collections, while a vice, only add to problems, worries, and overhead. Most collectors agree that their true reason for collecting was to mask their real life sorrows and give them something else to think about, care about, or fantasize over. While it may be fun to try to buy some happiness, the result is neither real nor long-term. I know it sounds like a cliché, but happiness must come from within, not from a collection of purchased items.

Opportunities Made, Given, or Taken?

Opportunities are not just created out of thin air. Opportunities usually arise from another person's sorrows. Someone has to lose in order for you to gain. The more and more our species thrives upon taking, the better the chances are that, one day, someone will be taking from you. Ultimately, one day, you will become someone else's opportunity.

"Opportunities" are created, not handed out. Opportunities cannot be wished for or blessed by prayer, and they cannot fall from the sky. Opportunities that come undeserved are called *luck*—the *luck* of a destined card drawn. Luck can also change with the draw of the next card. Hard work, perseverance, persistence, and smarts make for opportunities.

Pace yourself; it's a long race. Be smart and friendly and fight only when necessary. When fighting, first study the battle. You can be right and still lose. You can win, but will there be retaliation? Will one battle lead to a war? Wars never have winners, and they consume lots of resources and your life. Every action has a reaction, and sometimes the reaction is stronger than the action. Therefore, you better make sure that either the first action is a knock-out punch, or you may have to battle the war. Kids, I really and truly hope you understand this teaching, or if not, ask me to elaborate. I will not be personally financing your own vendettas and private wars. Fighting through my own has been more than enough. Many of a battle, I wish I did not engage.

To prove yourself right may cost more or cause you more trouble than it was worth. Satisfying your ego is expensive, so you better make sure your ego can afford the fight. My ego doesn't make any money. Most of the time, a battle is best fought by walking away, settling, or ending the aggression. You have no idea how hard it is for me to actually say such things, but in today's times, there is no place for my *barbarian attitude* of an eye for an eye.

The Past

Remember, when and where possible, put the past where it belongs and look to the future. Sometimes it is better to settle or walk away and live for tomorrow. Don't drag negative pasts into your future. Don't bring with you the trauma, drama, and negative energy. You want a future with bright smiles, right? Then why would you voluntarily bring with you the frowns and sorrows of the past? Bring forth the learned experiences and wisdom, not the continuation of what you are trying to move away from.

Learned experiences hopefully lead to better judgment. Unfortunately, at times, Life has us learn experiences from bad judgments! Just learn and don't repeat the errors. If you did learn, consider it a victory. Knowledge comes from trials and tribulations. Experience creates the master. Everyone must learn by hard lessons taught. At least with bad experiences comes new wisdom and a chance for future redemption. If you don't learn to fall, if you don't learn to roll correctly, you will never improve and advance. Parents should punish their child's bad judgments, not his or her mistakes. People need their mistakes in order to learn what they refuse to listen to. Knowledge is always power, prevention, and foresight.

Growing Old While on Life's Game Board

I am sure that each of you could write this book or chapters within it. We each have our horror stories, our turmoil to revel in, our challenges to bear, and our demons to face. We have all been the victim of Life's injustices, uncertainties, and unfairness. In truth, such stories will continue, and I'm sorry for that. Life sucks. As a comforting gesture, understand that Life sucking is not limited to you! We are all affected. We all suffer, and sadly to say, the older we survive, the greater our sufferance.

Mom, stop making me birthday parties. Growing old is not a blessing, as the golden years are a figment of someone's imagination or a lie we've perpetuated; shit brown would better modify our final years. Growing old means putting up with more of Life, only now you do so with an aged body and mind, little earning capacity, illnesses, more body hair, less teeth, needed medicines, lots and lots of body noises, increased gas, and all of the secondary problems that age brings to us, such as being easy victims for criminals and disrespect from our youth and an inability to properly care for ourselves or even drive. You know Life is laughing its ass off when you must use Viagra! People still tell me that I look good; the problem is that they then follow this up by throwing in, "for your age!"

Speaking of age, youth is definitely wasted on the young. If I could only have my youth back with the experiences and wisdom I have earned. You too! It's like that sports car you always wanted. I am now old enough and finally have the ability to purchase that sports car, only now I'm too old to enjoy it.

Chapter 4

WHO HAS THE ANSWERS?

I do not proclaim to have the answers. Hell, I don't even know the questions. What I do know is that each and every one of us repeatedly asks, "What's so good about life? Why are we doing this? What is this about?"

We live a life riddled with crime, wrongdoing, immorality, indifference, contempt, arrogance, envy, jealousy, intolerance, sickness and disease, poverty, filth, suffering and indignation, hunger, war, famine, love and loss, lack of love, extreme life changes, betrayals, costly mistakes, unfairness, unreasonableness, idiots, lawyers, politicians, alarms, steel bars across our houses and businesses, fear, insanity, laziness, the Ice Capades, unfair competition, reality shows, Dick Cheney, George W. Bush, Obama's economics, taxes . . . I am sure that you can add to this list.

I wouldn't know where to start telling my life stories; I don't know whether I should, or whether you even care to listen. I have had just about the most rounded life of anyone I know, but still, Life has permanently left its mark on me. I graduated with honors and had an amazingly successful law career. I earned many career awards and definitely kicked ass for my clients, if I do say so myself. I have traveled the world and experienced more than most people can dream or even know to dream of. I have learned how to start from the ground up, and most importantly, I have learned how to persevere.

However, I have experienced times of real trouble, times of tremendous sorrow, times of great depression and incredible injustice, times of need, and times of personal and family humility and crisis. Life has shown me the danger and evil of humanity and the Dark Side. Life has demonstrated its power and ability to conquer, to take, and to knock me out of the heavens when I thought that nothing could. You must be nice to people and treat everyone with respect. Not everyone is your friend, but that doesn't mean you have to walk in contempt. If you don't want to be nice, then stay home. Never proclaim yourself as *beaten* or a *victim*. Use the experience to better yourself and better those who did you wrong.

I have seen just how quickly your "good" friends leave you when you're no longer buying drinks and playing with go-fast toys, when you no longer have contacts and connections to burn, when you're suddenly not a *limelight* magnet. I have learned that living in the stars should be only a dream for the youth to strive for. As you age, it is best to reach only for inner happiness and peace of mind. Until and unless Life bites you in the ass a few times or one good time, you won't actually understand these teachings. Life necessitates experiences if you are to know reality. Venture into the world and get bitten; it is what you are supposed to do if you want to live a real life. When your wounds heal, do things differently the next time you run into a similar situation. Most of your troubles probably came from your ambitions, lust for conquest, envy or greed. Pigs get fat, and hogs get slaughtered. Curb your ambitions now, or they shall be your downfall. I have learned not to allow my words or actions to venture outside my home, and when I feel a need to scream, yell, gossip, or share sorrows, I talk to my horse. My dog has gotten tired of listening and only wants to smell his ass.

Age should lead to wisdom, and wisdom should help you handle Life's stress. Wisdom learned from Life's hard lessons is a true education. With age, I no longer talk about lofty ambitions and dreams. I enjoy what little I have left and do not strive for more. Maybe it is because I now understand the pain of losing it all or knowing that Life will take your dreams and loves from you. No longer do I care to make lots of friends and, in fact, shy away from almost everyone, as I recognize the inherent dangers of people. I've watched as my supposed friends acted like vultures in my time of need.

Kids, I am now telling you, as a father, friend, and defense attorney, stay away from social networks. Nothing, and I mean nothing, good will come from exposing yourself to the world. Your postings, displays, and information shared will leave you naked and preyed upon. One day, the information you thought was great to post and brag about will be turned against you and probably by your *then* best friend or soon to be ex. You just never know when or how things will come back to bite you; thus, assume it all will.

A street education is still an education. We are all shaped, molded, and changed by the experiences we encounter. It is not just that we learn from these experiences; we actually adapt to them. Experiences are who we are and what we are to become. Do yourself a favor; stay away from dogs with fleas. It is not fair that Life judges you for the friends you keep. I understand that you are not your friends nor are you responsible for their actions, but you will be unfairly judged for them regardless. Guilty by association—definitely not a fair concept, but we are judged on perception; yes, that is not right nor is it fair, but Life sucks.

For instance, you are with a group of friends. Some within this group smoke a joint. Cops come. Everyone is arrested, including everyone who had nothing to do with the marijuana. Guilty by association, and your life just turned into hell where you must now prove your innocence as the presumption is you are guilty.

Here is another example. Your buddy cheated on his girlfriend. You said nothing. It comes out later. Your girlfriend now accuses you of the same, through association. Because you said nothing about what your buddy was doing, she insists that her accusations "must be true"; after all, you were hiding something! Yeah, yeah, it's illogical, but perception makes for a reality.

Don't Confuse Ambitions with Ego

If what you seek is your own fulfillment, stop feeding your ego or materialistic desires with notoriety. I'll tell you what; every time you believe you are *the last coke in the desert*, go and try to order around another man's dog; that should deflate your ego.

Building wealth when your lusts are spending it just as quickly is very difficult. Material items go onto your loss accumulation or asset depreciation sheet, not your asset balance column. Yes, your accountant may put your fancy sports car on your tax return's asset sheet, however, that expenditure is really a loss. You purchased that expensive car for ego and notoriety. You don't need a sports car; in fact, it is impractical with your family of four and eighty-five-pound Labrador retriever.

Why do you feel a need to own such a large house? The upkeep, the costs, the security provisions—you are a "target," but your ego thinks you are great. I once had a case where I defended a home security company. A South Beach millionaire, a show-off and arrogant SOB, came home one night only to find waiting intruders. The police found him dead, stuffed inside the trunk of his fancy sports car in his garage. His lifestyle got him killed and unceremoniously stuffed into his trophy car. Moral of the story: Don't attract attention to yourself; it's better to be seen but not heard.

Notoriety may bring you attraction, but that is different than fame. Attraction draws the attention of all kinds of wrong people. Everyone wants to bring down a target, alleged friends included, as long as it gets them where they believe they need to be and what they believe they need to have.

Do not be a fame seeker or name-dropper. Anyone who is anyone will not be impressed. When you try to impress others by dropping names, what you're really doing is taking the intended attention or importance away from yourself and giving it to the person(s) whose names you dropped.

Do not seek *fifteen minutes of fame*. The truth asserted is irrelevant. People just love to believe the story, the lies, and the gossip. If the lie is said and repeated, it must be true. What is worse is that we reward these people (liars, cheats, and extortionists) with book deals and money. Even if what these fame seekers were saying were true, we should not reward people for ultimate betrayals, breaches of loyalty, and loose lips. So much for honor and manhood. I say, "Make them walk the plank."

Chapter 5

WITH HORROR AND TRAUMA, YOUR SENSES OPEN

I have been told that I am in need of some serious psychological counseling. Even I recognize my imbalance, but as Life would have it, I can't afford a good psychiatrist. I guess I'll just remain a little crazy; but then again, what is *normal* these days and who proclaims to be normal? None of my friends.

I wish I had learned earlier in my life that peace of mind is worth more than anything money can buy and that money cannot buy peace of mind. Chaos in your life will bring trouble. Money will bring complications. Excessive materialistic purchases usually mean that you are not really happy with what you presently have or who you are. Steadiness may be boring, but it comes with less troubles and worries. Steadiness also signifies stability.

I have heard it said that one's eyes don't change. Wrong. Look into my eyes now and compare them to photos taken a decade ago. I have grown wise to my experiences and have learned much through my mistakes, lapse of judgments, and the world around me. My eyes used to be a soft blue. They are a hard, royal blue now, squinted with stress. I now ask myself more questions to which I have no answers. I guess I better keep learning.

We forget that we humans are part of the animal kingdom. Many of us are best suited to roam the jungles, mountains, and fields alone or to mix with others in small communities for purposes of mating, hunting, and protection. Some of us are not meant to mix and mingle at all or are to integrate from safe distances or for short periods of time. As part of the animal kingdom, we all must recognize the inherent dangers and the sudden charge of the lion no matter how great your mother told you that you are. You must be conscious of the fact that your ego is a hindrance and nothing more than a feeder system to your stupidity. It is your arrogance that will mask your weaknesses from yourself, causing you to be eaten. Life will show you that the smaller animal—the one who had less and looked uglier, the one you picked on and terrorized in front of others so you could be a big shot at his or her expense—will be the one who later shits where you were eaten. What you did while picking on this person was to teach them how to prepare for their survival. That poor child who you humiliated had to learn to survive in ways you did not know. The bullying caused some to be eaten yet sharpened others to survive and bare a hatred that drove them to their successes and hopes of sweet revenge.

You, on the other hand, obtained and maintained an attitude: "I'm king of the world. I can do what I want, with whom I choose, and nothing will change for me." Well, my arrogant and ignorant king, Life will teach you that there is always someone bigger, brighter, stronger, and faster. Life will show you its teeth just as the game dethrones you. Your arrogance either will become your weakness or will blind you to your weaknesses. Kings get lazy, complacent, and fat, while the hunted become hardened, fast, conditioned soldiers all without even realizing it.

Survival Requires Conditioning

It is within your best interest to learn how to handle, manage, and care for yourself, so as to be as independent as possible. Leave your attitude for the mirror. Understand that every enemy made is an enemy looking for revenge. Life shall cause you enough pain; you don't need others intentionally looking to add to your misery. Unfortunately, the game has Life's Dark Forces running around looking to *cause you unjust pain and misery*, so if you have to fight, at least be prepared to do so and be creative about how you do it.

If your mother didn't tell you, then allow me. Bullying others or humiliating others will only make you feel bigger in your own head; everyone else will really think you are an asshole. Bullies have no real friends. Most playground bullies go on to become foot soldiers in the wars controlled by those they had picked on. By the way, did I tell you that, in this new world, the *geek* gets the girl? That girl who the school bully was trying to impress grows up to want things, expensive things. That school kid *geek* grows up to become the president of a computer software company or an officer in the military—the same officer who sends the bullies to the forefront of the battle. The bully screams from the gunshots, and the girl the bully once tried to impress screams the name of the bully's commanding officer, now a *geek* with power, privilege, and benefits, while in a chic hotel in Paris! Poetic justice.

Becoming a winner is much like a good game of football. You don't know who the winner is until the last second ticks off. Life has too many interceptions, too many fumbles, too many blocked field goals, too many quarterback sacks, and too many behind-the-line-of-scrimmage tackles. So don't be scared of difficult times and never think of yourself as a loser, as Life will take the game down to the last second. The one who wants to win the most probably will. Think creatively, think outside the box, and always look to control your situation and environment. You do not have to be the most physical to win, as proven by David beating Goliath. There are so many ways to persevere without sheer strength; endurance, smartness, creativity, strategy—to name a few.

The game board causes not only your position to change but that of your fellow players. It only takes one good roll of the dice for destiny to change. Time will change all—for better or worse or maybe both. But it will change your life and allow you to reinvent yourself—hopefully, armed with newfound knowledge and wisdom.

Play Nicely with Others

Make the most and best of every situation. If you don't want to play with others, no problem, so long as you do not isolate yourself to the point of being antisocial, dangerous, or a psychopath. Do not flex your muscles unless you have to, as you should not threaten unless you are absolutely willing to engage if your threat is called out.

Maybe global warming and natural disasters are Mother Nature's way of *cleaning house*. We haven't had a cleansing of the planet since Noah and his ark. It's time to line up two by two and prepare ourselves for the Second Coming.

Life's Allowances

Let's face it; Life *sucks*. Like death and taxes, you can count on the following:

- You are going to have more bad days than good days.
- Being bad is easier than being good.
- You are not the only person who feels up against the world. Stop talking and role the ordained dice, as good and even better days will come.
- As you age, you will learn the difference between fiction and reality. While growing up, you stopped believing in Mom's stories about the tooth fairy, Santa Claus, and the Easter bunny. As you wised up, you learned that Disney World is only a place for tourists. We do not get to live in Cinderella's castle. You do not control your own destiny, as too many variables and unknowns come into play.
- You are going to encounter Life's injustices and inequities the moment you step forth. Anyone not yet a victim has not interjected him or herself into the real world. To gain more, one must take chances. Chances, however, are just that. Chances are uncertainties and opportunities for both good and bad to occur. Let's hope for the best.
- The Dark Side does not care whether you are the best person in the world, the most honest, or the noblest; in fact, these traits make you easier prey, as you will least expect the dark forces and the troubles they deliver. You can take measures of protection and preservation, but that doesn't change the fact that you can still fall victim. You may fall victim to a crime, to uncertainties,

or to a lie. Either way, you attracted Life and now must play defense in spite of all your goodness.

- You will cry more than you will laugh. So when you do laugh, make it a good one.

Once you stray into the real world, both the Dark Side and the Light Side of the Force will attempt to recruit you. The Light Side of the Force may offer you an education, a home, a family, a sense of stability, and noble causes. It is doubtful that the Light Side of the Force will provide you with any early or easy rewards. The Light Side would most likely tell you that, if you work hard, are good, persevere, and do unto others as you would have done unto you, you will one day be rewarded. The Dark Side's seducement promises a quicker and easier lifestyle—the consequences of which may be more than you bargained for, and there are no take backs.

The Dark Side of the Force will undoubtedly take a different recruitment tactic. The Dark Side will usually tempt you with fast and easy rewards, lavishes, undisciplined actions, and unbalanced fun. Such sexy provocations allure many into the Dark Side. It is hard to beat sex, drugs, rock 'n' roll, fast money, and bling as seducement. There is *no* such thing as free, fast, and simple. I promise you that the punishment and penalties for this behavior will outweigh anything gained—even the sex. You must think "what if," before you conduct yourself improperly. As with physics, every action has a reaction, and you will have responsibilities for your behavior. Nothing is worth the loss of your liberties or an unwanted pregnancy. Don't let Life teach you this lesson; please learn this from others who have already aged and not as the result of your own hard knocks.

Chapter 6

EARN DO NOT TAKE

The Light Side of the Force requires you to earn your gratification, not simply take it. Earning anything in Life requires time, energy, resources, and dedication. In other words, earn by working, sharing, and caring. The rewards and satisfaction are worth such efforts and shall be yours.

Be smart, use your sense of logic and self-preservation, listen to your instincts, learn from your mother's warnings, be distrustful, and learn to walk the streets. Men, I have found that a good woman's instincts are so much better than ours. Listen to her. Don't try to outsmart common sense. As Ronald Regan said, "Trust but verify." By "verify," I actually mean touch, taste, smell, and see what it is you are verifying. I cannot tell you how many times in business people have offered me money that turned out not to be theirs or shown me proof of funds that were nothing more than fakes and computer mock ups. Don't be afraid to take your verification to the next levels, and don't be afraid or embarrassed to ask. If the other side says no, you will have quickly proven your suspicions without having to waste any further time. If they have what should be their qualifying proof, they should not be afraid to show it.

Stuck on a Negative Space

Don't you hate when you are feeling completely depressed and others try to comfort you with thoughtless expressions such as:

- Come on, it's not that bad.
- Life's too short to sulk.
- It will get better; don't worry.
- There is a lot worse.
- It could be worse.

Real-life issues require so much more than kind and well-placed words of advice. Troubles or problems with money, housing, family, job, career, health, death, sorrow, disease, or with one's children require action, not talk. Talk doesn't pay the bills, and it doesn't cure the illness; talk actually winds up causing aggravation and frustration. Talk opens wounds rather than closing them.

Help by doing and knowing and not making this person beg or lose any more dignity than he or she already has. True help comes in finding or making solutions. You are smart. Figure out this person's troubles. You don't need to embarrass him or her further. A true friend or family member is there for you no matter what and is willing to help regardless of the issue as long as this friendship or family link is not abused. Even that rule is not set in stone, for there are times during which familial bonds or true friendship must take some abuse if that is what will ultimately help. A true friend or family member is not there to add to your burdens; rather, he or she is simply there in your time of need.

Only give advice if it's asked for. When someone is already suffering, the best words are words of action, such as, "Don't worry; I will cover you," or, "Don't worry, as I will definitely help in any way I can. How much do you need?" Even words such as, "I am here for you in every way emotionally possible," or, "Don't say more; I will help," or, "I know just how you feel," are action words. Words and phrases such as these are magic to a person in trouble. If you have a solution, just act on it and don't create an opportunity for the pride of the person who is suffering to get in his or her own way. Give advice later—after he or she can breathe. Always remember, when you do something nice for someone else, forget about it; when someone does something nice for you, it's a return favor in the making.

Life's Dark Forces Will Find You

Life is undeserving of our reciprocal love and positive outlook. We are forever faced with unwanted challenges, fears, gut-wrenching uncertainties, and broken dreams. The longer we live, the bumpier the road becomes. Ladies and gentlemen, this is true living. If you are a person who views Life with optimism, in spite of knowing all of this, good for you. You are much more of a spirited person than am I. I may live a bit lonely and depressed, but it sure beats the drama caused by shutting one's eyes to Life's evils or riding an emotional roller coaster.

Life brings problems directly to you, whether or not you are the cause of those problems. No matter what you do, no matter how good and true you are, Life comes to you. You will be blamed for things you didn't do; you will be tempted by Satan himself or herself; and you will be wrongfully punished. The only common sense that makes sense is that there is no sense.

Imagine driving alone on the highway. You are cruising at a safe speed and minding your business. Simultaneously there is one of Life's Dark Forces driving in another vehicle catching up to you. Wham! This driver of terror now involves you in an auto accident. You are now spinning across the highway out of control.

You are involved in an accident—targeted by Life. The wreck knocked you into other cars, injuring other people, and now you are being sued. The driver for the Dark Force of course has no insurance and no assets, so the lawyers (emissaries for the Dark Side) just made you the primary target, not because it was really your fault but because you have the money. In chaos, you are now the perceived *bad guy* and hated by the injured and their families. Life Sucks.

Life's Dark Forces will wreak havoc with or without your help. Don't help the cause by feeding the monster. I have been targeted on many occasions by those who want to steal my perceived *good fortune.* Extortionists have sought to take advantage of situations in order to make an easy buck off of my hard work. They call this "opportunity." The decision or ability to stand your ground and fight against these opportunists is yours to make. Sometimes, regardless of what you personally want to do, Life limits your choices. Battles require resources, and sometimes Life doesn't provide needed resources to the *good guys*. In real life, the good guys don't always win.

Good Times versus Bad Fortune

Bad fortune is having you or your loved one's health turn for the worse, losing your house and having nothing in the bank with which to feed your family, losing a child, or losing any ability to recover from a long fall. Hang on, cowboy; eight seconds is a long ride, and you are almost there. Keep things such as your opinions always in perspective. Don't cop a spoiled attitude in the face of others; it's not pretty. Always remember, if you can stay the eight seconds, your chances of reverse fortune are that much closer.

Life causes fortunes to be won and lost and takes us on crazy roads, over obstacles and over bumps. Life is a roller coaster of both sorrow and joy. *We are defined not by our crying but by our laughing.* The faster you dust yourself off and rodeo forward, the better your chances of persevering.

In spite of all the punches and kicks, I think one of my saddest realizations was when I decided that having supposed friends was too expensive and dangerous. I began to shed my supposed *friends* faster than water evaporates in the Arizona desert.

I learned that true friends are those who don't cost you anything. These are the people who are there for you at any time; don't care about your money; and don't want anything from you except to help you in a crisis, to share good conversation, and to ease your journey across Life's game board. Good friends don't care if you call, show up or not, or buy them a shirt when you travel. A friend is there to make life a little more bearable, not to give you more aggravation. *What a friend wants is reciprocation.*

It Must Be Your Fault, as It's Not Mine

It is easier to blame others for your own shortcomings. Why take credit for losses when you can blame others? Our system of "justice" allows for such accusations. The system is not *just*; it is just a system. Lady Justice is truly blind, blind to justice.

People are, by nature, jealous, in need of scapegoats, envious, irrational, greedy, liars, maliciously contemptible, and ill willed. People prefer to take shortcuts; look for the easier road to fortune; and, of course, fail to take responsibility for their own wrongful actions or inactions.

Ladies and jellyfish, drop the egos; drop the failure to take responsibility for your own actions or omissions. Do not blame others where blame doesn't belong; look to only yourself. Accept the fact that you are not perfect, that you were incorrect, and that you didn't have the Midas touch or a crystal ball, and take responsibility for misfortunes, the same way you would have taken responsibility and bragging rights for the fortunes had they occurred.

I also want you to understand that not always in life is there a winner and a loser. Sometimes shit just happens, and blanks are shot. Sometimes you lose for winning, win for losing, or an unexplainable result is reached and you can only claim good luck or bad luck. If shit should just happen, the cards are dealt as they were, or the roulette ball lands on a green hole, accept it and move forward, knowing and understanding that even this result was part of the associated risks, as small as they were, and others should not be blamed.

Today's society has no honor, no conviction, and no true sense of right. Today's legal system protects the wicked and taxes the innocent. I guarantee you that, in the days of the *Wild West*, people wouldn't dare fault others for their own wrongdoing. If so, it only happened once, as a bullet probably resulted. Those days are needed again. We need desperate ways to right wrongs, as our system does not work. We should not be limited to supposed help from others or the so-called justice system, especially when Life didn't provide us with sufficient resources to utilize those routes or wait them out.

I have been wronged, and it has cost me plenty of money, my family, and more crying than I can mention, and for what? The agony never stopped. Thank God I had some money, help, and resources. I feel so badly for those being wronged who do not have the money or resources to fight back with. If my world was rocked, I cannot imagine the despair and frustration those less fortunate are feeling. It must feel like a cowboy stripped of his six-shooter and heading to a gunfight. If the justice system does not work or does not work for those short of money, it is a travesty that our society does not allow you to take control over your own problems. As politicians have lots of tools and lots of money, they do not understand nor will they fix the legal system's defects. Those without will continue to be without and shall remain frustrated, cheated, and wronged.

Chapter 7

EXTORTED

A few years ago, I had a small group of some morally incorrect people begin to extort me. When I refused to pay them, as there was no legitimate reason to do so, they vowed to cause me harm. Not willing to be extorted and believing that the law would protect me, I told them to fuck off.

This was now six years ago, and I'm still paying for this decision. A bad settlement would have at least allowed me to continue forward and positively in Life. I would still have my family. Well, that is hindsight, and I doubt I could have paid the extortion anyway, as I was not as wealthy as these extortionists perceived and couldn't give away what wasn't mine to give. This story is going to be the subject of another book, screen written for TMI Pictures and slated for a TMI movie production coming soon to a theater near you.

For those extortionists out there, a lesson is at hand—extort by asking for small money. If you ask for too much, the person you are trying to extort will undoubtedly react by telling you to fuck off and lawyer up, as you will have left him or her with nothing to think about but getting at you and no choice regardless as they don't have that kind of money to give to you anyway. Realistically, you only gave the people you are extorting, one choice, which is to fight you.

Chapter 8

A TRIBUTE TO LIFE

I am sure that you have your own books to write. Each of you has experiences and stories that have shaped your lives, dispositions, and personalities. Many of you have gone through enough to realize that Life is more about trauma and drama than it is about fun.

I raise my beer in salute of Life. I salute Life—neither for its good nor its bad but for how Life molds us into becoming the person or people we are. I salute Life for strengthening us and turning lambs into lions, so that we can all rise to the challenges we must face. Raising my glass, I ask that you please repeat my motto:

When I am in a drunken mood, I gamble, fight, and drink. When I am in a sober mood, I worry, work, and think. When my moods are over and the time has come to pass, I hope I am buried upside down so that you, Life, well you can kiss my *ass*!

What's Life?

What's Life? Life can be everything and anything, depending upon how you look at it. Life is sad, Life is mad, and Life is at times being glad. Life is about troubles, problems, complications, love, joy, happiness, and whatever you can make of it. Life can even be about *The Cat in the Hat*. It's everything—half full, half empty, challenging, safe, dangerous,

29

scary, and happy—all encompassing. We can all agree that Life is disheartening, disappointing, and bumpy. Life can also be as sweet as a kiss that fills your tummy with wonderful, tingling sensations. Living is a journey in which we are pawns for Life's amusement.

We are blinded by our own arrogance. We cannot imagine a power greater than ourselves. We cannot perceive ourselves as a pawn on someone or something else's game board. But we are just that.

Chapter 9

HERE OR THERE?

Is it possible we are simply a creation for someone or something else's enjoyment—a pet for a big alien kid? So many in our society believe in a God; then why not believe in the theory that our lives are divinely contrived and controlled? Divinity will only let us get so powerful and allow us only so much control. Perception and imagination take over where our true control runs out.

Reminiscing, I realize that I was never in control. Life was always biting me in the ass somehow or somewhere. If I dared to drop my guard or smile too long, *wham*. Reality check! Life is a sadistic "MF," and we are its bitch.

I have lived and experienced enough to know that we should never count on anything. The only common sense we should count on is that there is no sense at all. We cannot be sure about our love or the love of our partner. We cannot say we are secure in anything, as we cannot control the world around us, not even the world of those who share our bed. We cannot even plan or gauge our existence or tell of our death. For the most part, these are all major and material events that are outside of our control and should humble and humiliate our egos.

We can agree that Life is not fair. Fairness lives in Disney's Magic Kingdom. Fairness comes from those Disney stories Mom reads to us.

Oh, if living could be a Disney fairy tale, "what a wonderful world it would be. Yo Ho, Yo Ho, A pirate's life for me".

Unfairness is really more of what we encounter. Unfairness, in fact, is our test of survival. Have I lost you yet? If so, well, that's Life. Let me give you an example. A good friend just reinvented his life and business. He was feeling positive. His new business model was sellable, and in fact, he had investors. His girlfriend was making him happy, and his kids, from his first marriage, were unusually quiet. Life was good. Wham! No, I mean *wham*, as he hit the floor, face first, collapsing from a heart attack.

Okay, he gets saved, operated on, and given a second chance. He had to improve his lifestyle by lessening his stress and eating healthy. All right, there is nothing wrong with these life changes, and they are understandable and no doubt good for him. Sucks that I lost a good drinking buddy, but again, that's Life. So he becomes alcohol free, exercises more, guilts his girlfriend into more daily sex, and begins building his new business. Just when things are looking as if the rebound shall be positive, *wham* again. What? Now a pacemaker is needed. Everybody is telling him how lucky he is and that he will soon be as good as new with the inclusion of his newly installed bionics. I told him to ask for one with a USB port and blue, blinking lights. He is alive and recovering, and remember, Life was still good, just with less drinking and less red meat. Worries should be over.

Not so good, for when he went back to the office, he learned that his investors took over his new business and kicked him out. A post visit to his doctor for more tests ensued. The tests revealed two forms of cancer eating away at his colon and prostrate. The end.

Mom, are you still going to tell me Life doesn't suck?! I mean, what is the point? How can this be fair? This is a true story and happened to a very close buddy of mine. Why bother to continue playing Life's game, when Life is playing so devilishly?

Living equals surviving. Life scares me. I am sure that each of you have asked yourself, at one time or another, just who is playing who? What is our purpose? Our destiny? Why are we playing at all? I assure you that Life is playing you and that you are part of its amusement. The fact that we cannot identify Life is an additional scare. We suffer from the fear of the unknown; someone or something more powerful than we are. We can't see Life. We can't fight Life. In truth, we are somewhat helpless, and to those such as me, that is highly frustrating.

Religions were created from or premised upon people's fears of the unknown and the lack of control we have over our own lives. At least my dog is ignorant to the fact that he is only a dog. Ignorance is definitely bliss. As Forest Gump says, "A box of chocolate is just a box of chocolate." Less, in fact, is more. The less we think, the less we strive, the less we know, the simpler our existence, the better off we are. A dog's life isn't so bad.

Life can be exemplified as a magazine. I want the magazine, but it is expensive and comes twice wrapped in order to make it difficult to open and impossible to read before purchasing. Its pages are fragile and tear easily, so those who try to open the wrapping too quickly or improperly or to just to sneak a peek without paying will be foiled by the pages tearing and the words smearing. This magazine costs ten dollars! I, however, only have two dollars. Sucks, huh? No, this is Life, and neither of us will ever be able to afford it or prematurely review it, and we will certainly face difficulties when we try to open it. Hell, the worst part is that, after paying for it, opening it, and journeying through its pages, we may not even like it or find it fulfilling. It may be just awful or disappointing. Pretty packaging, no real content—welcome to the game. Ready to keep playing?

Did I Tell You That Life Sucks?

I have edited and edited this book, as there are so many examples how Life can and does suck. I say this from personal experiences, many of which I shall not write about as they are none of your business. I also have too much to say regarding my mother and yours, but that is to come! Just kidding, Mom. I love you. And by the way, Mom, thank you. I don't say it enough, but I'm thinking it. My mom was scared to death that I was really writing a book that bad-mouthed her. Love you, Mommy. Relax, I would never do that to you *publically* and do not have anything negative to say about you regardless. Do you still believe everything you read?! Keep reading mom.

On a side note, as my own children rarely listen to me, maybe they will understand from this book what I have been trying to teach them. I doubt it. What child actually listens to his or her parents or understands the lessons the parents are trying to convey <u>at the time of the teachings</u>? Most kids must learn through hard knocks. As long as they learn, we, as parents, should be thankful. What child these days actually sits and reads a book? I would have to digitize these pages and put in music videos just to get my kids the slightest bit interested. Life is now an MP4 player or Apple something or other.

Experience comes with age, and for many of us, we must get our fair share of knocks and bruises before we really learn from our experiences and create change. By the time this happens, we have burned through our youth, which is wasted on the young. Now older, we cannot do what we once wanted, either due to physicality or simply the lack of desire.

Seeking Happiness

Finding a partner to travel around the game board with is wonderful. It is even more wonderful if you can call this partner your best friend, your spouse, your confidant, your everything. Very few of us can actually find someone who helps make our lives easier and raises the level of our gamesmanship.

Life is not defined by your material possessions. Life cannot be bought. Don't get me wrong; money helps. Money can make your playing time easier, but understand that having more toys does not mean being happier. Having materialistic items does not mean money in the bank. In fact, materialistic items are possibly a loss, maybe an asset, but not liquidity. Dollars in a bank account make you breathe easier and should give you greater peace of mind. Expensive toys have expensive upkeep, maintenance, and security issues. Cash is king, and please, please, please don't let anyone know about it if you have any.

Money can also cause multiple, opposite effects. Money can tighten you up; in some people, it causes a hording effect—the need to see and corral as much of this green paper as possible. I have seen lots of people get addicted to seeing their dollars grow. They stop spending altogether in order to bathe in their Benjamins. They become outright tight. Others become paranoid, believing that everyone wants to steal from them.

Monetary possessions are only vices, and believe me, the joy doesn't give you the bang for your buck. In the end, it is really your family—your spouse, your children, your parents, your siblings, and all the positives that you wish for them—that matters. However, don't spoil them; spoiled loved ones become tremendous enemies, overhead, and headaches. The trick is to use your wealth to create balance, understanding, and appreciation.

A solid marriage is a difficult proposition, one that is more difficult to achieve than a job or career. For many, living is too hard to go about it alone. You need a partner, a lover, a person who you can sound off to and work in conjunction with, a protector, and betterment. This must be a mutual and respectful relationship in order to work. A spouse who is a scrub won't work out in the long run. The working spouse will grow bored and resentful. A quantitatively non-contributing spouse will wind up with nothing interesting to say, tired, complaining, and bitchy, and again, a loss of interest between the couple will occur. Your partner must bring something to the table, that their other recognizes as tangible, and walk together with you through thick and thin. If not, you don't have a partnership, and you just invited hurt to befall you. In that case, it will be better to have walked the red dirt road alone. Having alone time is nice too, and given how long we now live, solitude and companionship must ebb and flow.

The Couple

The couple is the cornerstone of every family and a safety net within Life's game. A strong couple is the foundation of a healthy family, a healthy mind, and peace at home, which is where you need to be, as well as being the safest place on the game board. Most families make a fundamental mistake by placing the children ahead of the couple. Husbands and wives due do this, but it is wrong. You and your partner must find a way to keep your partnership first and to be true to and with each other. To keep the family strong, the couple must first be strong. Your emotions and feelings will transcend directly to the rest of your family unit.

I'm not going to give marital advice, but I will tell you that you must keep your eye on the ball. You must care for and cherish your partner. Your partner must be your lover; your best friend; your caregiver; the parent to your children; and, most importantly, your *it*. He or she must be someone you do not want to hurt for any reason; your connection must be one that defies physics. Anything else is merely for show and not worth the expenditures, such as a new car or trophy wife. These things are pretty, new, expensive, and exciting for now, but at the end of the day, they are only toys, untested, untrue, a distraction, a cost, and absolutely not necessary. If your arrow is not aiming at your lover's heart, then you have reached that stage where solitude becomes necessary, at least for now. Life and your living require change. Everyone's timing is different, but life does go on and time does heal.

Should you and your partner form a pack, Life and its obstacles become much easier to handle. You now travel around the game board as one. This does not mean that you will not have times where you are at odds with your spouse, but you make it work. You can be mad or upset at each other, but that doesn't mean that you have to stop loving each other. One of the biggest mistakes any couple can make is allowing your lives to grow apart. Do not go off on your own independent roads. The farther you each stray from each other, the easier it will be for Life's Dark Forces to single you out, divide you up, and conquer you. Temptations will find you, especially when you're on a divided road.

Lastly, remember that relationships are work. Relationships are a work in progress and require just as much time, attention, and resources as your career. The same applies to your family. What happens if you fail to put in the effort at your day job? Well, the same will happen to your relationship, marriage, or family unit. Every married couple has several simultaneous careers, and you must understand and work at them all. Nothing is easy; such is Life. A spouse and family are a challenging career—maybe more than your day job, given the dynamics. Careers and jobs change and so does marriages; again, that is Life should you live long enough.

Children can and will come in between you and your partner if you allow this. Children want to be number one and center stage. Children will later grow up, leave the nest, and create their own problems, which you will be inevitably dragged into. If you are lucky, only you and your spouse will remain in the nest. Hopefully, you will have saved enough energy for a second honeymoon.

Life will throw everything possible against your partnership and your unity. Life will tempt your partner with theories of better or greener pastures. Life will tempt you with that twenty-year-old hottie. Do not give into Life's betrayals and false desires. My father used to say, "There is no end to nice." I wonder if my mom brainwashed him into believing that! However, it really is true; there is no end to nice. Just when you think something or someone is beautiful, wham, your eyes lock onto the next. Best advice, be happy with what is proven and leave the rest to fantasy and dreams. Remember, you can always be replaced as well. Not me of course, nor my F-150, but you can definitely be.

Should you allow Life to break up your partnership, today's love will become tomorrow's greatest enemy and the largest heartbreak you've ever felt. Just ponder this thought for a moment. Life had you fall in love and marry and maybe even blessed you with children. You shared your life with this person. You made kids with this person. You even raised a puppy. How is it possible that this person would later do everything possible to destroy you? While you cry, Life laughs. Life is a psychopath. What is just as bad is that the laws that govern our lives will allow your destruction simply because you lived long enough to desire change. You are not going to win either way. Life will tempt you, show you some sugar. And then, after you take the bait, it will rot your teeth out. Life sucks, and you can blame life, Mom, or my friend, Matt. In fact, blame my friend Matt. Go ahead; wipe your feet all over him. *See, Matt, I told you the glass is half empty.*

Chapter 10

LIFE'S BETRAYALS

A. Money doesn't buy you happiness.

Money definitely eases living. Problems can be bought off. While money brings peace of mind, it does not necessarily buy happiness. Life, as part of its sadistic gamesmanship, has made money a necessity to living, and the acquiring of money unevenly and unfairly between people.

The wealthy have fame, fortune, glory, and lots of people doing things for them. The wealthy are coddled over and envied. However, their portrayed happiness is for the camera's benefit. Look how many of these supposedly happy few wind up in trouble. Whether it be due to drugs, messy and well-publicized divorces, jail time, career crises, bouts in and out of addiction centers, having their own children taken from them, and on and on, Life catches up with them—proof that we must gauge even the fortunate few like an iceberg. Look not to the top but deep underneath the icy waters, where Life's Dark Forces cower. I am reminded of a saying, "Don't trust your lying eyes." Even though the rich and the famous may look happy and successful, you really don't know what's going on with these people's lives.

B. Betrayal from those within cuts deeply.

Within the confines of your loving partnership can also be felt the greatest of Life's pains—betrayal, discontentment, loneliness, grief, unhappiness, loss of faith, and inner sorrow. You should be able to feel and sense your partnership—a certain oneness. You should be able to read and be in sync with your partner's vibes, feelings, emotions, thoughts, and beliefs. The pain of Life is best demonstrated when you sense something wrong with your partner. Before your warning radar went off, you thought everything was okay. Now, you sense the change, the unexpected difference, that fly ball high into left field. You tell your partner that you love him or her and get no answer back or get an "I love you" that is a little less sincere then you'd hoped for. Worse, your partner allows you to make love, only instead of feeling reciprocal passion, you feel that this exercise was nothing more than *pity* sex or *obligation* sex, or "shut up and leave me alone" sex. At least Life allowed you to get sex; that doesn't suck. See, my book is positive and inspiring. I'm talking about fifty shades of something.

Those feelings you have—that emptiness, that worry, that uncertainty, that helplessness—are the feeling of Life's pain and the greatest of hurts. Life has done this to you merely to wipe that smile off your face (probably because you just had sex), as you shouldn't be so happy while on the game board. The game is meant to make Life smile, not you. Remember, you are Life's entertainment.

Life will ultimately take your loved ones from you. This is not limited to your better half. The *taking* can be in the form of death, illness, brokenness, flight, or misery. Why did this happen? This was not deserved. You didn't sign up for this. You tell yourself that bad things are supposed to happen to bad people, not the other way around. What kind of Life does this? For what purpose? Is it natural selection? Survival of the fittest? WTF. By the way *WTF* will be the title of my new book, due out soon.

Maybe we are all just born into this world with a timer and a curse. I don't know the answers, and I have a lot more questions, but what I can tell you is that Life sucks. Let me remind you—the good die young. The good are taken off the game board; be happy for them. The good no longer feel Life's pain; nor do they have to put up with this game;

good for them. As for you, the pain persists. I guess you aren't as good as you believed you are. Stay off of Santa's lap.

What about when tragedy occurs to a child? Nothing is worse. How can Life allow such a thing? To do something to a child, Life must be inherently evil. Life throws twists of fate. Life always pushes us and tests us, but why does it do so to such extents and extremes? These extremes go unchallenged, and when finally answered, the extremes are met with opposite versions instead of middle ground. As examples, extremes are, you laugh while I cry, Democrats versus Republicans, conservatives versus liberals, men versus women, parents v. children, and yin versus yang. Why can't we all strive for a middle ground? Why must we all constantly challenge others instead of challenging only ourselves to be better? Why do we always make living so damn difficult? Living is tiring—another job. We have made living so difficult that, in essence, most of us live to survive, rather than living to love.

I reiterate that Life must be inherently cruel and evil. You can say that the curses running parallel to your life are tests of faith, but I don't believe so. Faith and divinity should not need to go to such extremes as causing emotional, permanent scarring, loss of loved ones, or grave personal harm or sacrifice in order to prove a point. No, there is a Life out there—a sick, sadistic, MF of a Game Master.

However, if you want to remain positive, then you should believe the universe maintains balances. For each negative, you will find a positive. Maybe the negative you are facing was dropped on you for a positive reason you have yet to recognize. However, now you are playing into the theory of divine intervention and God's plan.

Really and truly, why must lessons be so hard to learn and punishments so severe? And what if we still don't understand this *lesson* Life wants us to learn? Does Life continue to punish the ignorant or those with a little less brainpower? Where did our species go so wrong? Where did our teachings and upbringings go so awry? We exist in a broken society. We see it, we discuss it, and we debate it, but at the end of the day, we do not fix it. We are broken, and we recognize it but do nothing to cause real change.

What about when shit just happens to us—when we find ourselves in situations we didn't mean to get dragged into or, quite frankly, don't know how we even got there? Why must Life punish us when we innocently involved ourselves in troubled situations? Where is Life's compassion, understanding, forgiveness, tolerance, and just rewards? Life has none of these attributes, and it gives out second chances rarely and randomly; in short, Life sucks.

I have found lectures against alcohol to be a total waste of time and underlying medical rationale. By drinking, I have discovered that alcohol is actually part of Darwinism or "natural selection." Once, while shit-faced drunk, I was watching the Discovery Channel. The program showed the migration of the African wildebeest—a thousand-mile trek through lion—and crocodile-infested territory. Through this entire ordeal, natural selection was prominent and proven. The wildebeests who fell to the back of the line due to age, sickness, inability, or tiredness were the first ones picked off by the predators and Life. Well, the same must apply to my brain. *Cheers* character Cliff Clavin, who apparently saw the same Discovery show as I did, sought to explain this point to Norm, in an episode of *Cheers*. Cliff says, "Well you see, Norm, it's like this . . . A herd of buffalo can only move as fast as the slowest buffalo, and when the herd is hunted, it is the slowest and weakest ones at the back that are killed first. This natural selection is good for the herd as a whole, because the general speed and health of the whole group keeps improving by the regular killing of the weakest members. In much the same way, the human brain can only operate as fast as the slowest brain cells. Now, as we know, excessive drinking of alcohol kills brain cells. But naturally, it attacks the slowest and weakest brain cells first. In this way, regular consumption of beer eliminates the weaker brain cells, making the brain a faster and more efficient machine. And that, Norm, is why you always feel smarter after a few beers."

I would like to come back to the theory of divine intervention. Do you believe in some kind of higher being? Do you believe in a God? If so, what do you make of this God? Do things happen for preordained reasons, or do they just happen?

With the passage of time, enough will happen that you can find a meaning or means to justify anything. For example, my wife and I purchased a property in order to develop it. Due to reasons of horrible weather and permitting issues, our project continued with delays. We had told each other that we would resist, as long as possible, having to borrow bank money for this project. When things started to look good enough for us to begin thinking about really pushing the project to next levels, including borrowing bank money and collateralizing the land and the project, we got into unexpected litigation. We again slowed down the project and stopped talking to the banks. In fact, we had a meeting to possibly sign for a bank loan the day after we got served notice of the litigation. What timing, what luck; or could this have possibly been some type of divine intervention, as we did not go to the bank meeting and take on a bank debt due to the bullshit lawsuit? If we had taken the loan and then gotten sued, along with a collapsing of the world's economy, we would have certainly lost the land and project. We were saved.

We can claim that divine destiny saved us from the strong possibility that we would have acquired an expensive bank construction loan, which, given the sudden downturn in the economy, would have financially destroyed us. Was it just luck? Or was it just how the game played itself out—time allowed enough events to transpire and one could point to a magnitude of reasons for what happened?

Chapter 11

WHERE DID ALL THE COWBOYS GO?

Few are left to fight against wrongdoing, inequities, and injustices. We merely trod along within the herd and ignore what is happening to our neighbors. It is almost as if we've stopped caring for anyone but ourselves. We hide within our herds and pretend that nothing else matters or that the world won't find us. But what if your herd is being led to slaughter and you are right there with them?

One of the ego busters of living in a herd is finding out that not everyone likes you or you don't like everyone. This is okay, and we must accept the fact that we cannot please everyone and that not everyone will be our friend. Do not live your life trying to please everyone. Just be nice and don't worry about everyone else, as everyone else is not worrying about you.

Not everyone needs to gain access or be accepted by the herd. Moms forget that there are wolves in sheep's clothing, mixed within the herd or trying to enter. These wolves are certainly looking to eat us and then our moms. The herd will take care of themselves, and moms should wait to go out of their way until the need arises, not before. Their preemptive actions will go unappreciated or underappreciated, and Mom will develop a standard she'll be expected to maintain later. Thus, Mom, please leave well enough alone and let the herd fend for itself. When the heard is in trouble and needing you, I am positive they will call out to all moms. Until then, let your babies grow up to be cowboys or cowgirls.

It is also okay—even better—to be different. People should be individualized and have their own personas. Whether you're a loner within the herd or just different, individuality is okay and makes you special. Be true to yourself and don't worry about others. Others don't have to live within your head, so don't let others influence who you are.

We all have issues! Call it baggage or call it trauma, drama, or chemical imbalances; we all have been changed by Life's ordeals. I promise you that, tomorrow, you will be different and changed from today. Life will do that to you. For good, bad, or indifferent, you will be a changed person and, if seen, hopefully understood.

The herd will also teach you not to play both sides of an argument or issue. Don't try to remain neutral. Don't try to be liked by each member of a feuding side. Neutrality only works for the country of Switzerland, and even that privilege has its uncertainties. In any regards, we are not Switzerland and cannot claim neutrality, whether it is true or not. In the end, the person who tries to play in the middle becomes hated by all. The fight and troubles get brought to you, regardless of your side, so you might as well pick one. Also, remember that a friend of an enemy is an enemy; that an enemy of an enemy is a friend.

Friendships are like first marriages. It's hard to find a good one or one that will last. In fact, I know many people who refuse to even attend first-marriage ceremonies. For the most part, first marriages do not work. With that said, the degree to which we still support them is amazing. Why, then, are we still filled with happiness for our daughters on their first wedding day, especially when we know they'll end up being stuck with small kids and we'll have to financially support them all after the marriage tanks? Or do we cling to faith, tradition, and the silly notion that our kids have found that Blue Prince or Princess our moms told us exist in this Life?

Please tell me that you didn't let your kids get married because they were bored, "in love," pregnant, or high on life. Better you tell me that they got married because, not only were they in love, they had found partners who strongly complemented their strengths and weaknesses and vice versa, each partner bringing a value added to the marriage. A marriage is a partnership, and unless both partners are creating a balance, the love will wear off; the respect for each other will fade, and Life will throw at them temptations.

I believe that in today's financially difficult world, women need their own careers, topics of conversation, and competitiveness in the household. In today's seriously troubled financial marketplace, a stay home spouse does not cut it. I believe women are capable of besting men in a wide variety of careers and intellect and should not limit themselves or use their children as an excuse, as good as an excuse that it may actually be, and stay at home. Neither men nor old-fashioned traditions should stand in the way of a woman being all that she can be. A woman's job in a marriage is also harder than the man's. Men are designed to *go hunt*. A woman has the difficulty of keeping her man at home. That is a lot of pressure upon women. I tell my daughter that she is to take care of herself first. Her future needs to be independent and intact and cannot be reliant upon any man. If she wants to be in love, marry, and have her own family, she must still maintain her own freedoms, independency, and controls, so that if her man does *go out on the hunt*, she can still survive without skipping a beat and without having me reach for my shotgun. Obviously, I am being extreme and talking a little smack, but I hope you appreciate the point I am trying to make for the benefit of our daughters. No man is better than my daughter, and no man will turn her into a housewife, where her entire life and living is dependent upon him and his commands. I teaching my little cowgirl how to fend for herself and that of her family should she need to.

In today's busy society, our lives have become nothing but work, financial issues, more work, problems, and then there are the kids. We misconstrue "associates" with friends. Friendship has taken on too broad a meaning. Associates aren't true friends, but these days, we tend to call them friends. I believe this change or this new way of viewing companionship is because we tend to have less social skills, less socialization, and less knowledge of what a true friend is. This is a shame and how one gets hurt. A friend is someone we really know and can lend some trust to. A friend shouldn't bare malice or harmful intent toward you, whether today or tomorrow and even if tomorrow you are no longer friends. A friend should be there to offer his or her assistance no matter what. An associate who we treat as a friend possesses too many risks as his or her character and baggage are really unknowns.

How many best friends have we had over the years? The definition of a "best friend" is only a friend who hasn't yet screwed you over or vice versa. How many of these so-called friends have we gone to bat for when they have needed our help? How many of you have suffered alongside your so-called friends? The truth is that, in this generation, we shed "friends" so quickly that the term has no true meaning. Have we forgotten what being a true friend really means? Is it that we don't really make true friends or that the term "friend" has been lessened to mean someone we happen to talk with?

The concept of not knowing what true friendship is anymore, even transcends to how we purchase and consume. We don't purchase anymore for longevity, where we have to provide tender love and care to that which we cherish. We instead lease, so that we can dispose of thirty-six months later, and since we know our new item will soon be gone, we don't provide the necessary tender, love and care that we should. Therefore we don't respect our property or respect the property of others. *Respect* is therefore a characteristic on the verge of extinction.

Today's society is disposable. Everything we eat, everything we do, and everything we buy, we quickly dispose of. Paper cups, Styrofoam plates, plastic silverware, take-out food, best friends, friends, spouses—we throw away everything. If society is disposable, then so too are our standards for friendship, family, loyalty, and honor. This is disgraceful. This is a strong reason for wanting to be alone. This is a powerful point evidencing that our society, values, and ways of current life are simply fucked up. Where have all the good cowboys and cowgirls gone?

Today's children know nothing about *loyalty* and *brotherhood*. Commitments, loyalties, sacred bonds, family—are all concepts left to be researched in a *Godfather* movie. To a large extent, our society, police force, laws, and legal system have helped destroy these admirable qualities. Instead of honoring the fellow who wants to remain true to his or her word, we deal out punishments to those wanting to remain true, more severe than to the actual wrongdoer. We turn people into snitches and liars due to enhanced punishments and legal, extortionary tactics, and actually praise people who tattle and make up excuses for those they snitch on.

Friendship requires loyalty, which should be a trait our society rewards and respects. Now just the opposite is true, as loyalty has been taken out of the equation, given that a true friendship does not really exist. As a species, I'm afraid that we have lost our social values, as loyalty should be commendable and admirable. We have become so greedy and "I" oriented that we only care about ourselves. In today's schools and programs, loyalty and commitment are discouraged. The *powers that be* reward us for snitching and tattling. WTF. These *powers that be* demand our loyalty; however, they demand loyalty to them and for themselves only. Our parents, teachers, and government fail or refuse to acknowledge that loyalty is an aspect of the truth and not only must we be loyal to ourselves but to our own judgments, beliefs, friends, family, and those who we have allegiance to. Again, loyalty should be admired and rewarded, not punished.

Hiding our true loyalties is another form of dishonesty, and instead of making us dignified and honorable, hiding our loyalties shames us into the role of a traitor. The irony is that the powers that be are the biggest crooks of them all and only want to stay in power. The government is the largest of Mafias and worse, as government, unlike the true Mafia, has no loyalty, no sense of family, no hard rules, and no real understanding as to how we must play upon the game board and take care of those within our neighborhood.

The days where men fought alongside each other for glory, brotherhood, and guts are gone. Like the cowboys of the old West, honor among thieves has gone the way of the dodo—extinction. What is learned in confidence must always stay in confidence, which is the "code" of men, the West, and pirates alike. To break the code should be met with severe punishment.

Today's loyalties are bought instead of earned and, sadly to say, bought cheaply. With the street thief, you don't expect loyalty, but you would from your friends. Along with friends who are here today and gone tomorrow, so are your secrets, commitments, and loyalties. Today, if you were to need help, who would you ask? Who would come to your rescue? The answer is few if not none.

Part of the problem may be that this generation doesn't know how to build a friendship. This generation only knows how to sit and play video games. Without hard sweat, blood, and tears, true bonds cannot be formed. It is true that, when you have gone to hell and back with someone, the bond generated is lasting. Everyone is great in good times. It is the bad times that build character and let you know who is besides you. Walk through the gates of hell as boys and come out as men.

A generation forged on principles of "give me, get me, buy me" will not last. Children need to learn how to socialize, build their own toys, play stickball in the streets, stand up for others, show each other respect, and earn and share. There is something special to be said about *old school*; it is a shame it is no longer taught. If commodary is not learned and appreciated then we are only creating a generation of lone wolves.

Social or Solitary

Maybe we are not meant to be such social animals but more solitary. Peaceful solitariness allows you to take more responsibility and credit for your own actions, while attempting to keep yourself out of harm's way from others.

Just look what has happened to a national hero, Michael Phelps, after his 2008 Olympics wins. Months after breaking all the gold medal Olympic records, he attended a party. And why shouldn't he? He is young and single, has fame and fortune, and deserves a good party. Well, our hero just happened to take a bong hit at a party. During his "feel good puff," some asshole thought it would be cool to use a camera phone and post the photos. Well, lessons learned for Phelps, as Life bit him pretty good for his indiscretion. His partying buddies turned out to become Life's Dark Forces, as their actions cost him sponsors, a bout with fear of the criminal justice system, lots of negative press, problems with the team, and good pot wasted.

Looking for Cheat Sheets

Funny how we are all atheists until times of trouble. Atheists, my ass; just wait until shit hits the fan. Then it is "Oh God, why . . . ?" or "help . . ." or, "please," or "I swear . . . ." We look to the heavens and prayer books for answers when things are not going our way or when we are guilty of something and then thank the heavens and prayer books if things begin to improve. Neither prayer nor your calls to God had anything to do with your next move, as God must be busy.

I am completely flabbergasted that people actually would have the audacity to maintain this type of "religion when needed" attitude. If you are not a believer, then why pretend? If there were a God, why would he help those who only come to him as a last resort and not true followers? Why would God help those who are guilty and only looking for a get-out-of-jail-or-trouble-free card? A little disingenuous, don't you think? How many guys have looked to the heavens and begged God to make sure she wasn't pregnant. "God, please. God, I beg you. I will always use a condom after this." Yeah, until the next girl is beside you and you are trying to work your magic before she comes to her senses and runs.

"Religion when needed" will not and does not work. It will get you nowhere, and if she didn't get pregnant, it is not because of prayer but because one of you simply isn't that fertile. But hey, thank God for small favors. Maybe Life doesn't suck so much after all and maybe you need to loosen your britches.

New Chapter

Physics and Life's game card turns fortune. Stupid you to believe that you can have only good cards. There would be no Vegas.

I will go on record saying that we are *not* in control of our own lives. Take for example something that you do every day. Take your driving. I know you are the safest driver and never have had an accident or at least none of which were your fault. However, you cannot control the driver next to you. You cannot control Mother Nature and the tree that just fell in front of your path or the dog that ran in front of your car. Your control is, in fact, very limited.

It is not even limited to your safe driving, as I once had an associate who literally had a heart attack while driving and continued into a building. If you cannot control Life's events, if you do not know what will happen next, then how can you even think about controlling your own destiny? Party on, dude.

Chapter 12

WE BECOME PRODUCTS OF OUR ENVIRONMENT

We are groomed from our environment and become a product thereof. Crime does not affect a person who grew up in the University of Hard Life the same way it does someone who grew up only in the Halls of Yale.

Our environment molds us. We may be born with a silver spoon, or no spoon? A child has no control or any say as to his or her placement, but it will surely affect his or her life. The same children will have totally different judgments, reasons, actions, reactions, and perspectives based upon which crib they were raised in. No fairness, no justice, no sympathy, just the reality of Life. Depending upon the crib you are placed in, you can either ask Mommy for that new iPod or steal one. Our directions, motives, inspirations, needs, survival senses, rationale, reasoning, and logic are all molded from our childhood, upbringing, and environment. In large part, this is a matter of pure luck. The rich kid envisions Life as being grand. The child in the streets might envision stealing that *grand*. The cards do differ, and after the street kid steals the rich kid's iPod, the street kid has his moment of joy, and the rich kid is traumatized. In the rich kid's world, this theft is a trauma, whereas the street kid views this act of reality with a smile. The rich kid gets his mommy to buy him a new iPod, while the street kid has no mommy and must wait until he finds an opportunity to strike at your new model. The rich kid gets by asking and the poorer child gets by taking. The common element being both sets of kids have a need to receive; it's how they receive that differs.

It is so easy to judge and so easy to dish out negativity without putting yourself in the others' circumstances or seeing their actions through their eyes. What I'm trying to clumsily say is that, in today's society, we judge too hard and give punishments that are too severe for the crime. We don't fairly evaluate circumstances, backgrounds, experiences, and each person's rationale.

Take a child out of the ghetto and provide him or her with a minimum of stability and watch as the child's decisions and judgments change to reflect his or her new reality. The better the conditions, the easier our survival; our perceptions and decisions change. It is so easy for people with money to say they wouldn't steal for food when they don't know what it is like to go hungry. The person with hunger issues doesn't have many choices and, therefore, a different reality than those who don't know what it is like not to have meat for dinner. It is too easy and hypocritical for us to say, "Well, that person should have gotten a job," when we know it wouldn't be us who would hire him or her. In order to get a job in today's environment, you still need to have certain minimums. You need proper clothing, a proper appearance, a proper place to live, communication, transportation, proper hygiene, a cell phone, easy access to the Internet, Microsoft Word skills, and various other talents. The poor souls in the streets are doomed, and thus, in their reality, survival depends upon a different set of skills. As the rift widens between those who have and those who have not, so will our societies' troubles as a whole grow. Note, that neither the haves nor our politicians are doing a thing to fix this troubled issue, as they live behind large walls and security guards. Those who have, preach against self-protection and guns in the streets, yet I always see their bodyguards or security forces with their semiautomatics strapped to their waists. The *haves* are so hypocritical; unfortunately there are so many of us that just can't see it.

Hypocritical Culture

From September 2008 through 2009, we watched as the United States government bailed out industry after industry—none of which I owned, of course. We destroyed our fundamentals of capitalism by performing material acts of socialism. We showed the world just how hypocritical we are. We not only let down the world's free markets, we let down ourselves as a country. We bailed out the rich and powerful at the expense of the majority. Our politicians lied to the masses, having them believe that faults and blame lied not with government, but, if not for the government intervening we would all lose what was left of our jobs. Not true, and a discussion best left to another book. In fact, because of government, we have fewer jobs, less industry, and the fastest-shrinking middle class and shrinking access to money in the world.

The tax payers gifted high-powered corporate America with a trillion dollars while getting nothing in return. Our tax monies were legally stolen from us because the powers that be willed it, but in truth, they were stolen. I don't know about any of you, but I didn't consent to my tax money being utilized for the benefit of world corporations and the banks that have never given me anything—not even a toaster when I opened my bank account.

The banks still did not increase lending or put liquidity back into the market. After the banks received our monies, just the opposite happened; they took liquidity out of the market, cancelled everyone's credit cards, sued everyone for foreclosure, and added even more bank charges to our monthly overhead. The powerful elite did so well that they even convinced the government to continue to give them money—to loan them money at an interest rate that made it almost free and allowed themselves to reinvest it and make more money, all off of the blood, sweat, and tears of those poor taxpayers they are now crucifying. The taxpayers got completely shafted. The government allowed big business to take our tax money while still not paying its fair share into the same system it is bleeding. But that's Life, and it sucks.

Just makes you want to pay your taxes doesn't it! Such fiscal *irresponsibility.* I want to see if our politicians would use their own personal money toward the matters on which they so freely spend ours. I have no doubt that my tax share is higher in proportion than that of our powers that be, and I don't make anywhere near the type of income they do. It appears a good way of researching this issue further would be if everyone reading my book now buys ten more copies and has their friends purchase copies as well so that my income can rise and I can begin comparing with our powers that be. See, your contribution is a research project and worthy of a tax deduction!

Washington still doesn't get it; without liquidity in the marketplace, the middle class will never benefit. The country, as a whole, cannot grow financially without the means of providing the population with access to capital. The institution of credit is now a joke. When I had a job, I was very responsible with the payment of my bills. I had good credit. When I lost my income, my credit went down the toilet. I am still responsible for and still desirous of paying my bills. However, without work, without liquidity, it gets a little difficult. In order to fix the country's financial woes, the issue is not simply the payment of taxes, but providing the majority of us taxpayers with access to liquidity and working capital. Americans want to work and want to be successful but need the tools that appear now to be bestowed only upon the social elite.

With liquidity, you and I can purchase, we can grow, and we can have opportunities that level the playing field. All we should want is a level playing field. Then let the best man or woman win the end run. No matter what, taxes can't be paid if you are not making enough money to both survive and pay them. Banks must be forced to give back by ways of credit and loans to those who bailed their asses out. We should have let them fail; it was so wrong of government to hold them above the rest of us and, worse, use our money to bail them out so that they can foreclose upon us.

I'm not a Harvard graduate, but it would seem to me that, had the United States government spent those same trillion dollars within our own country's infrastructure and used it to clean up poverty, the streets, crime, and afforded opportunities to those who were left stranded, we, as a whole, would have benefited much more than we did from bailing out failed private institutions that got us into this financial jam in the first place. Our streets would have been cleaned up, the crime would have been dispersed, and people would have new jobs. Welfare, unemployment and Medicaid claims would have diminished, and new and more people would be paying taxes and, consequentially, giving back to the country. Mortgages and credit card debts would have been paid, and the banks would still be lending. New pride in our country would have been instilled. But no, Life throws irony into our faces, as our powers that be did not help the constituency but helped a different set of crooks, which wear fancy suits and know how to return favors with reelection dollars. The cruelty to this irony is that the reelection dollars being spent are the same monies taken from us hardworking taxpayers to begin with. So those who should have gone bankrupt did not, as they took our money, leaving the bankruptcy system for us less fortunate.

Of course, no one from Washington asked me, but I would have given all US citizens enough money to pay off all their nonspeculative debts. That would have been about one-third of what the government gave to the Wall Street crooks in suits. With all our nonspeculative debts paid, we would have all benefited and the middle class would have continued on a healthy footing. Taxes would have been paid, our treasury would have been replenished, and we would have been on a true road to recovery, not just a road where the rich got wealthier. Another sad irony is that the government has made the rich wealthier intentionally and then campaigns against the wealthy, saying that they should give up more.

Chapter 13

SHARING IS CARING

S haring really is caring. With sharing comes rewards. One can do a whole lot more when resources are joined. Sharing is like creating a pizza. Individually, we only have slices. Together we have an entire pie. Sharing also builds social skills and allows for us to work together to form a solution. By working together, we can solve and resolve issues that alone we would not be able to solve. Sharing allows us to combine resources so as to gain strength, knowledge, and positioning.

I would explain to my kids the necessity of sharing each and every time we were in Toys "R" Us. If they would only share, they would have double. If they would only share, they would have access to so much more than their own stockpile. If they would only share, they could collaborate and decide what interchangeable toys to get so that they could mix and match. If they would only share, they would not have to keep asking of me for more.

Children, listen to what I am saying as the reality of living is very much like going to Toy "R" Us and how you select your toys.

Chapter 14

SOCIETY NEEDS ITS PREDATORS

Predators hunt for survival. Predators also perform necessary evils. Predators eat the sick, weak, slow, and disorganized. Society remains stronger as a result.

What amazes me is how society looks at, views, and opines about these types of predators or carnivores. New, younger, stronger predators are always on the rise and hungry. Those around predators either fear them or want to be associated with them; they want to be them, want them jailed, or want them gone.

Others aspire to be like these aggressors. People are attracted to this showing of muscle, strength, and aggression. People allow themselves to be bought, fed into, and aligned with these conquerors in spite of better judgment. At some point, these followers will get turned upon and eaten. Listen up, folks, I understand that people like to align themselves with power, wealth, and glory, but recognize these simple facts:

1. There is no end to someone better, stronger, prettier, or wealthier. Remember even Bad, Bad Leroy Brown eventually lost, and he was from the South of Chicago.
2. Your alignment with power-driven people means that, every day, you are part of their fight and struggle to stay in power.

Once you enlist, you are enrolled, and getting out usually has a higher price than had you not gotten in at all.

3. You are but a glorified soldier, whether you recognize this or not. All soldiers must learn to shoot and get shot at.

4. Every soldier eventually dies or gets injured on the battlefield. The more you expose yourself or the longer you play the role, the greater the likelihood of your own demise. And for what?

Chapter 15

THE LEGAL SYSTEM IS NOT A JUSTICE SYSTEM

I would tell clients of my law practice that we are all guilty until proven innocent and that we are all innocent until we run out of money. The system works better for those who can afford it. The system may not be meant that way, but it costs money to play. This statement is true whether in a civil or criminal context.

Let's examine the criminal system, as it is the system we are most fearful of, especially as it is this system that can take away our liberty. The government employs prosecutors who start out as nothing more than young lawyers, fresh out of law school, looking for trial practice on the taxpayers' dime. These young, ambitious prosecutors probably care more about their end game, which is their trial practice, then about your guilt or innocence. Most young, ambitious prosecutors don't care that they are playing with the lives of you and your family, and are not taught or instructed to care. They are willing to work on the cheap, for the government, in order to get the trial experience that will one day fetch them bigger dollars. You and your troubles are but a learning experience for these youngsters' grandeur plans of trial practice and career building.

If prosecutors cannot find private employment, they get caught up in their prosecutorial role, which is simply throwing people in jail and not concerning themselves with the guilt, innocence, or mitigating factors of the accused. It doesn't take long before these career bound prosecutors become single-minded and forget that they are there to protect the innocent, not to appease those who yell the loudest, carry the biggest stick, or are part of law enforcement. Everybody in a law enforcement role should be required to fully understand the plight and sorrows of the accused, so that they have a balanced perspective regarding those they are trying to crucify.

An accused—civilly or criminally—has very little protection against false or malicious persecution. Where did our safeguards disappear to? The jury should be the final safety net, not the first one before a trial and, arguably, the destruction of one's life and that of their innocent family. Where sufficient legal proof does not exist, the law should not allow the claimant to proceed. Politics and laziness should not be allowed within our system called "justice." Prosecutors must be allowed to dismiss cases or have a third party constantly screening the evidence as it begins to come to light, not taught to turn a blind eye toward truth, justice, and the American way. Prosecutors should be a safety and an independent cog between law enforcement and the cruelness of the legal system. Today's prosecutors are sadly nothing more than law enforcement. Many, if not most, prosecutors identify themselves as law enforcement and say that their job is to prosecute, not determine guilt or innocence. Yes, my dear friend, but as a prosecutor, your job is to independently evaluate evidence and prosecute only those who you honestly believe broke the law or committed the tort you are formally accusing them of. Your job is not to use the weight of the government and the trial skills you developed on the money taken out of the tax system to put a person through the hell of the legal system just because you can. You know better than anyone, the unfairness and inequalities of the legal system, and you should be held accountable for your actions, held to a higher standard of care, and made to judge the associated costs, attributable to the tax payers, with your need for further prosecution.

Trials are performances. Juries could and do convict based on the theatrics they are watching or on their preconceived notions or biases, as opposed to the actual evidence introduced. What I am trying to say is that Life is unfair, and our legal system will doubtfully safeguard us.

The constitution placed the burden of public safeguards upon the government, but the government seems to have missed this memo. Better to keep the citizenry ignorant and controlled than armed and intelligent. Hence, our government's hostility toward the Second Amendment.

The general public holds a misconception that police arrest people because they are guilty. Not even close. Police arrest people for a wide array of reasons, and lots of these reasons have nothing to do with guilt. Prosecutors prosecute people because it is their job. Many judges keep people within the evils of the system because it is safer for their political agenda. The problem is that most judges are former prosecutors, and therefore, it is just more of the same mentality and actions. If the guilt is not apparent, why drag the poor soul and his or her family through so much misery? Why make people take such a chance with their lives and the well-being of their families? If the law allows the court to throw out a weak case, then by all means the court should *do so*. Do not leave a person's life hanging in the balance. Why cause both the poor soul and the taxpaying public to endure the tremendous resources of taking a case to trial when it shouldn't be there to begin with? Why even take the remotest of chances that an innocent person would be found guilty by a confused jury because this defendant didn't have the finances or stamina to properly fight?

The other problem is that today's punishments do not fit the alleged crimes. Punishments are too severe and too long. Many people take pleas or settlements because the stress and continuation of the system simply puts too much undue pressure, influence, and illness upon them and their families. Not everyone can stomach the stress and finances associated with litigation or the crying from their family. Families always suffer from litigation—as the innocent always get hurt.

Judges are supposed to intervene and not allow any undue influences to come between the hard lines of the law and an accused individual. Everyone within the system knows that a *jury by their peers* is a misnomer. There is no such thing as a fair and impartial jury, and there certainly is no such thing as a true jury by our peers. The Constitution says we are to be tried before our peers, but the years have reshaped the definition of *peers*. Jurors are people who bring to the jury room their own opinions, biases, innuendos, misconceptions, and experiences. None of these precontrived or preconceived mental stimuli can be separated from the case before them. Everything reminds somebody of something. Sometimes the memory is a bad one, and thus, these negative feelings will spill over into the case against the poor soul being tried before them. News and media also play into the unfairness of the system; this is an undue influence, as most people stupidly believe what they see or hear in the media.

Law enforcement has the ability to arrest people for any reason, as long as they have "reasonable suspicion." This means nothing and everything. Reasonable suspicion is a catchall. Anyone, and I mean anyone, can be arrested and for all the wrong reasons—for trumped up "reasonable suspicion." Everyone has reason to be scared of such power.

Fighting the False Allegation

Defending the "lie" is one of the hardest and most costly defenses to mount. Life allows a simple, unsupported allegation to ruin someone's life and the lives of their family members. I would tell my clients that I was more scared about defending the carefully placed subtle misstatement than the obvious lie. Police and prosecutors know that people lie and should conduct an independent investigation on their own, looking for both the innocent and guilty evidence. They should not take the easy road, which is to simply believe and arrest upon an accuser's allegations or what I call "first-light evidence." *First-light evidence* sometimes is too easily obtained, if you get my drift—just too convenient. No one should so easily accept the lies, the maliciousness, and the falsehoods of witnesses or accusers. Today's mentality is simple—make an arrest and let the defendant's lawyer prove this person innocent. It doesn't matter, nor is it even considered, that lives get ruined in this process. Entire families are destroyed. A person's defense should not be left up to his or her finances and ability to hire a good lawyer and investigators. Life especially sucks for those not able to pay to play. The number of truly innocent people who have been destroyed because they simply didn't have the proper means to defend themselves against the government and its limitless tools is scary.

The Founding Fathers of the American Constitution purposefully wrote minimum standards by which the government must abide when weighing down on "the people." These words of wisdom came at a high price, as the king's army had been arresting the colony members for any and all subjective reasons and then hanging them. The Founding Fathers knew that governments could carry too much weight and had the ability to roll over people if not constrained by law and a system of checks and balances. These protections were premised on the philosophy that no innocent person should go to jail. Today, *we the people* have found every way to vacate or minimize our constitutional protections so that the government can maintain control. The Second Amendment's "right to bear arms and form a militia" came from the wisdom that a government fearful of its constituents would be a government always looking to please and do right by its constituents. The purpose of the Second Amendment was that our government would and should be fearful of its people, not that *the people* would be fearful of their own government.

And just as a footnote directed to our government: Causing a shortage in our ammunition, increasing the taxes placed upon our ammunition, or causing the price of ammo to increase is tantamount to taking away our guns and directly violating our constitutional rights. You are not fooling us; you are disrespecting the wisdom of our Founding Fathers, and you are circumventing the laws of this country. The right to bear arms, includes our ammunition. Yeah, I know, that's Life, and it sucks.

Chapter 16

ONLY THE STRONG SURVIVE

C harles Darwin proved that Life functions by evolution; "only the strong survive." We have improperly tampered with Darwin's philosophy of survival of the fittest, and at what cost?

Our society tampers with Darwinism, as both scientists and medical physicians would like us all to survive and grow old as Olympians. Why? We would keep the weak, deformed, sick, elderly, and viral all alive, and for what selfish purpose? We prolong agony in the name of humanity or maybe because of our own guilty conscious, self-acclaim, or ego. What type of life have we given to those who defy the laws of evolution? In the animal kingdom, those unfortunate would perish and, if lucky, in one gulp. The laws of nature maintain population control and availability of food sources, ensure the strongest offspring, maintain quality of species, and reduce the suffering of those unfit to continue within this miserable game of Life. Why are we seeking to defy the laws of nature?

The child who continues to swallow marbles shouldn't have children of his own. But we let this child have offspring and then seek to blame the schools or our Second Amendment when these offspring prove not to be the brightest. We can foresee this turmoil, yet we turn our backs to it. In the end, by allowing stupidity or conforming to it, we are no smarter than the boy who eats marbles; and we then have offspring of our own. Go figure and guard the marble bags, paint cans, and ammo. Hell, why not guard our spoons as well. By the reasoning of our government, because of spoons, I am eating more and gaining weight. I should move to New York City where I can be told how large my spoon can be.

By meddling with the laws of nature, we destroy the balance intended. Everybody's fucking with everybody, humans and evolution alike. We are destroying ourselves, our planet, and our wildlife and depleting our natural resources. We are decimating our economy, our children's future, and our relationships. And we are tearing down our morals, our goals, and our rights and entitlements. We have destroyed the way we live. Life, however, is pushing back in ways we don't yet understand and with forces with which we cannot reckon. Life is fighting back by making Life not worth living. Our good days are gone. Our happiness has left us. Our desire for antidepressants is great. We now coddle depression while drooling all over ourselves; pull the fucking plug, will ya?

If Life is hard for the young, healthy, and strong, can you imagine what it must be like for those less fortunate? For these less fortunate souls, Life must not only suck, it must be a living nightmare. Quality of life is a must in order to feel peace and happiness. Prolonging this less fortunate soul's agony is not providing happiness. I strongly doubt that these less fortunate people want to remain alive if given a choice. Even for those born healthy and strong, there comes a time at which they must give up or certainly want to. Everyone reaches that point in life.

Is it our ego or someone's allegedly high sense of morality preventing us from saying "enough is enough" and legalizing the possibility of pulling the plug? If we can't say "end it now" because of some third party's self-imposed morality, then I say "pull the plug" in front of them. These same hypocrites probably voted for legalizing marijuana. If these third parties outlaw your ability to check yourself out of the game, then they should be responsible for making and maintaining a better living for you. Watch how quickly these do-gooders change their morality when suddenly blessed with the responsibility of taking care of your smelly ass!

If a person, after conducting his or her own due diligence and failing to come up with a reasonable and achievable alternative, chooses to take his or her own life, we should not consider this a wrongful taking. After all, if you are religious, euthanasia is a refresh button of the sorts. Euthanasia refreshes you to your next path. Isn't it hypocritical for these third-party morality preachers to say that we control our own lives and destiny but we can't control the timing of our own "endgame"? Why not? And how dare others tell us this is wrong when they are not living in our shoes? It's wonderful when you are on top of the food chain and not allowing anyone else his or he chance, but for all the rest of us who are running for our lives and falling off of ladders, please, let us die with some dignity. For some of us, the reality is that living is too hard, too impossible, and not worth waking up for tomorrow. Don't you hate these arrogant and morally hypocritical assholes who impose their thoughts, beliefs, and opinions upon others while taking zero responsibility or providing any real help to those in need? It is so easy to preach to others when you don't have to feel their pain, sacrifice, or despair. Talk is cheap. Let's see what these assholes say about their morals, values, and rules when they are forced to step into the shoes and pressures of those who they are today judging.

It is somewhat hypocritical of me to talk in such a way. On the one hand, I am saying that life will change for us all, and then on the other hand, I am saying cut yourself loose. You are right; it sounds hypocritical. But we must look at people's reality and weigh the circumstances. Before prejudging someone else, we must understand his or her reality. We must understand each party's perspective of the life they are living. For those who are contemplating ending their gaming, I would say, "Wait; wait for the cards to be drawn, and your life to change." When your life changes for the better, you will have a refreshed perspective and be happy you put down the gun. Also, remember that it is your family that will suffer and be forced to pick up the pieces of what you left behind. But I do understand when a person can honestly tell him or herself, "I have had enough." "I've been dealt so many bad cards, my hole is so deep, that I don't care what good fortune card I may soon get. I can't recover or too tired to care".

On December 22, 2008, I was watching some Monday night football. It was a wonderful Bears vs. Packers game being played in negative degree weather at Soldier Field. Switching to the Discovery Channel during a long play review, I began watching a program about new medical technologies and their role in helping humans to live longer. I watched in utter amazement as two scientists now believe that, within the next decade, they will have not only isolated the human gene for "old age," but will have a way of countering or mitigating it. These scientists talked as if they just found the "New World." The new magic pill apparently is a derivative of red wine and comes from a chemical found in the skin of the grape. These scientists have already alleged to have been successful in animal testing, whereby they have doubled the life expectancy for mice and various insects, as well as found a secondary side effect, which is that this new pill can help control weight gain and actually can make you skinny without the need for diet. These scientists believe that human life can be extended up to three times! I kept watching, expecting to see these two sprout horns from their heads and change their skin color to red.

I don't know about anyone else, but the proposition of genetic immortality scares the shit out of me. We were not supposed to live longer then we already do and, in fact, already live beyond the years Mother Nature intended. Our medicines, fancy medical machinery, cloning, and the ability to substitute pig hearts for human hearts is all a direct challenge to Mother Nature and the laws of survival of the fittest. Playing God is a no-no, yet our arrogance has us do it anyway. We wonder why Life creates horrors such as viruses, hurricanes, earthquakes, fires, floods, and other acts of disasters. This is Mother Nature trying to level the playing field, as we keep interfering with her law of survival of the fittest.

If not for a great Chicago Bears game that I had to switch back to, I may have thrown my Bear's football at these imbecile scientists. These sadistic madmen actually believe they are heroes and are doing us a favor by prolonging our misery. Can you imagine that there are madmen such as these two geniuses who want to alter the human gene pool so that we can all play on Life's game board for another two hundred years?! Can you imagine having to worry about literally everything for centuries? Can you imagine the physical and medical strains your body will have to tolerate as you will now be prone to more of Life's ups and downs—especially the downs? Can you imagine what your needs will be and the fact that you will probably never be able to retire? It's bad enough that we have to support ourselves, our families, and then our children and their families, but can you imagine extending that to our great-grandchildren as well. Ouch. No thank you!

If humanity was destined to live longer, nature would have extended our life expectancy for us. Humanity would have evolved in some manner, the Holy Grail would have been found, the fountain of youth would have been bottled, and the US government would have either had the patent on eternity or be fighting over it with Mickey Mouse.

Everything in Life *costs* and costs in extreme ways, not just financially. In order to make a diamond polished, it takes the friction of Mother Nature. To polish humanity takes Life's trials and tribulations.

Chapter 17

BECAUSE OF KIDS

Most of us stay living because of our children. There is no better reason. But do you stay in a bad relationship because of them too?

I would bet that at least half of you reading this book have gone through a divorce. Many of you probably stayed in your marriage, beating yourself up and willing to live in hell for your children. I did, for years and years. I don't resent being with my children, don't get me wrong, but I do resent having to have lived in a state of mental torture because society has imposed its beliefs that parents must stay together, no matter what, because the kids need both parents under one roof. In fact, this is the worst thing that parents could do to themselves. Life is hard enough; you should not have to make it any more difficult by living where you either don't want to be or are not wanted. The physical and mental pain and stress you put on yourselves negatively affects you and your children. A couple that is not happy does not spend time at home or with the children, as both partners are desperately trying to escape being with their spouse. Unhappy people go somewhere to hide, only to return after everyone else is in bed. When unhappy parents finally do split from each other, slowly they too begin to smile again. Children see their individual parents happy, some for their first time.

Parents who are not running or hiding from each other spend better quality time with their children.

Don't stay in a bad marriage. You cannot live like that and owe it to yourself to try to have a life. In the end, if you stay, there will come a point in time when you just won't be able to take it anymore. You'll eventually leave, lash out, exercise really bad judgment, or self-destruct. It just becomes too much. Rip off the Band-Aid and end the torment; it's best for everyone involved.

After the divorce, there will be a substantial change in your living circumstances, but you will still be the parents of your children and still do your best for them. Accept your limitations. Do not feel like a loser if you can't do everything you or your children wish. You must explain to your children that your reality is theirs too. You must explain to your children that yes, even you, have feelings and they too get hurt. Accepting reality eases tension, frustration, and reason. Stick with and accept your reality—today's, tomorrow's, and the next day's.

You can't live your life through others, not even through your children. We all need our hearts to be warmed, to feel loved, and to enjoy a sensual touch; we need to feel positive, respected, and dignified. You must take care of yourself if you are to become a positive influence on anyone else. Find your own happiness and watch how it rubs off on your children and within your new life. Joy is not happiness; it is a moment of glee. Happiness must come from within; you must glow, and it must last more than a moment in time.

Life's questions and answers have no universal right or wrong. At day's end, the decisions and consequences of your actions are yours to make and endure (good, indifferent, or bad). Think things through before making rash decisions. Sleep on big decisions. If you can't sleep, find a way. Rash decisions more likely become regretted decisions. Every one of your actions will have a reaction and consequences. Think through and ahead as to what the possible consequences of your actions or inactions can be and gauge your decisions accordingly. By forward thinking and planning, you can actually change your future.

Chapter 18

WE WANT WHAT?

W hat is it we are seeking or want out of Life? Where has that "loving feeling" gone?

Inner peace comes when you are truly content. When you can close your eyes anywhere and feel as though you have just downed your third margarita on a beautiful Bahamian beach, "No worries, mon." Inner peace is a feeling of lack of pressures, stresses, or major concerns. It is when the world is leaving you alone and you have dropped off the radar. It's as if, the world has been lifted off your shoulders. It is when you can smile for no reason, when you have that *loving feeling* just because, when you wear wings on your feet and there is no music playing. It is like feeling in love for the first time.

Inner Peace

Wikipedia: The Free Encyclopedia says the following about inner peace:

> Inner peace (or peace of mind) refers to a state of being mentally and spiritually at peace, with enough knowledge and understanding to keep oneself strong in the face of discord or stress. Being "at peace" is considered by many to be healthy (homeostasis) and the opposite of being stressed or anxious. Peace of mind is generally associated with bliss and happiness.

My life's experiences have taught me that true happiness or peace of mind cannot be bought. Yes, money definitely makes life *easier*, as you can purchase *comfort*; however, you can't buy true *quality of living*. It also turns out that the more you purchase, the more troubles your purchased items bring, the more items you have to worry about, and the more your overhead and maintenance expenses increase.

Quality of life and quality of living are distinct. You can buy quality of life by purchasing the best of the best or purchasing comfort. Quality of living is the ability to establish peace of mind, serenity, and tranquility.

It is ironic that you can buy "comfort" when it's something you don't need to purchase if you're already living within your means, content within your reality, or have achieved a sense of satisfaction. I believe that the need to purchase is a result of an internal emptiness, dissatisfaction with the way your living, or a void that needs to be filled.

The happiest I've ever been came at the lowest financial point of my life. I was financially hurting, but my wife and children showered me with their love, warmth, and loyalty. I absolutely beamed with inner glow and realized that, as long as I had them, their love, and their support, none of the materialism mattered. My family proved to me that they did not need these items and that I shouldn't feel as if I have to provide them in order to be their father and husband. I could lose my Lexus but not my wife. I could lose a weekend house but not my son's smile. I could give up purchasing clothing but not the warmth of my bed. Truth be told, I had learned that I really did not need to purchase anything but basics, as my family found ways to be happy by doing little things. If we wanted to go to the mall, we went. Only this time, we would go and make fun of ourselves, remembering a time when we would buy just to buy and pay those ridiculous prices for such absurdities. Stupid us. We became healthier and began utilizing the outdoors, instead of the malls. Camping, barbequing, and hiking not only saved us money but, more importantly, it brought us closer together. We talked, we shared, we made fun of the rest of you, and we created our own world; and what a lovely world it had become.

To have quality of life, you really don't need much more than the love of your partner and family. I would venture to say that you can live without 70 percent of what you already have. You need 30 percent of your possessions; the rest is likely unused because it's either excessive or you're holding onto it for whatever your hang-up is. Ask yourself if what you want is really needed or just a spoiled craving. Look at the price of what it is you want. Do you really have the cash to make this purchase, or if you do, would the cash be better used in buying something that you really do need such as groceries or school needs? To my children, here is a novel idea: Save your money and wanted possessions; a penny saved is a penny earned, and it's amazing how fast those pennies add up.

Simplicity helps create an easiness and inner peace. The less you have, the less you must worry about. The less you have, the more you appreciate what it is you have and the more you will use. We must simplify and exemplify. We must live with less and want less, and if we want more, then we must learn to share.

The best use of your money is toward a product that you use and use over and over until it can't be used anymore. That is getting your money's worth. I have several pairs of cowboy boots; however, I always gravitate to my oldest and now ugliest pair. Why? Because they are broken in just right and are the most versatile and comfortable. Besides, they weren't always ugly, and I am loyal to them, as we have walked a lot of miles and stepped in a lot of shit together.

Shoppers are not happy people. Shoppers tell themselves that their purchasing is impressive to others and try to demonstrate or present an air of wealth and desire toward others. In truth, these folks only impress themselves, and nothing good will come from showing off. People will not only look upon you with distain, envy, or jealousy, but they will recognize your shallowness and emptiness. Besides, if you are ugly, it doesn't matter how expensive or designer that new shirt is; you will still be the ugly person in an expensive, designer shirt.

Leave off the Flash Adjectives

Let me also throw you a piece of advice. When talking about yourself or your belongings, leave off the adjectives. Try to minimize (or stop yourself from voicing) the embellishments. While embellishing may create an interest in what you are describing, remember that the interest you are creating may prove more than what you wanted to achieve. You can discuss your new car, but do you have to tell everyone that it is a Porsche or reveal its uniqueness? Why do so? Remember that the Dark Side has many alliances and members who also want what you have. The Dark Side wants your smile and whatever it is that is making you smile, such as that unique, never-before-been-in-an-accident Porsche.

It sucks to work so hard to acquire something nice for yourself, only so that Life can allow some Dark Side thief to steal it away from you. Life, in this regard, has taught me that, if you want something, you should go ahead and get it but shut up about it. If you want to keep your wife, when you talk about her, leave out the parts about her incredible beauty and inner qualities, her genius intellect, her sexual skills and flexibility, or her ability to suck a golf ball through a ten-foot garden hose. Don't give other people the desire to have and test what you are bragging about—to try out your wife or husband.

Life has also taught me to question my conversations in the first place. Why do I have to talk about myself? Why am I talking about my properties, assets, family, or travels? Am I doing so just for bragging purposes? Just as importantly, am I revealing too much about my personal life? Why does this third party need to know so much about me? Dangerous. Shut up and talk about the weather, and if you really want to appear as the nice person, steer the conversation to the people you are with and move them into comfort by talking about themselves and just how great they are! Let others talk and brag about themselves—after all, it's likely their favorite topic of conversation—and you'll gain knowledge about them. Besides, these others will have such a great time talking about themselves that they will go home or to the office saying wonderful things about you. A good listener is better than a great talker. Listen and learn.

Bragging is really only something you do for your own self-gratification and insecurities. Bragging does not impress others; it only turns others off. While important personal conversations may be had, be selective with whom you are sharing this information. Remember, even your spouse may one day become your greatest enemy.

Life will always put nice things in front of your eyes as evil temptation. Life has been dangling apples in front of men since the days of Adam and Eve. If you are already in possession of something or someone you love, stop, enjoy, utilize, love, and cherish that thing or person without wanting more. Life will always show you a new version of what you have or don't have, what you certainly don't need, and what is definitely not worth the trouble or acquisition costs. You must realize that Life shows you the newer or different versions in order to tempt you out of the sure bet. Life can allow you to win a Ferrari, but can you actually afford it? Do you need it? Do you really want this car? Is this car more problems than it is worth? Now that you have it, can you keep it? Now that you have kept it, do you wish you'd never had it? Life may laugh as you go bankrupt just from the associated insurance and gas costs or the special security features you must purchase because, of course, you can't shut your mouth. You brag to others on the golf course about owning a Ferrari, even while the car valets at the club are contemplating ways of stealing it from you and going through your personal effects inside.

Don't change what you are already happy with. Don't change what has already proven loyal. Loyalty is priceless and rare. Finding someone you can actually live with and someone who will not dump you when times are tough is a person who you stick to like glue. Don't change what is already purchased and still working. Don't swap the old for the new just because of the model year. Don't actually be so arrogant as to believe that the new model year is the right fit for a geezer such as you. Don't allow yourself to fall out of love or travel down different roads then your spouse. Love and relationships are hard work. It will not matter the model you are driving; there will still be work involved. Although the newer models may provide new thrills, they are more complex, unfamiliar, and require more work or maintenance.

The bottom line is this: If you are happy with something, *stop*. Don't look to change, don't look to replace, and don't look to try out the new product. In fact, *don't look at all*. Why look? Looking is only a way of teasing yourself, and it will only bring you trouble. The new is unproven and probably won't work out. And even if it does, this new model will grow old and troubled as he or she will become self-conscious that a newer model, just as he or she was, is around the corner.

Life does not allow temptations, such as new models, to come for free, and the cost is always high, both financially and psychologically. The *sampling*, if it pertains to cheating on a loved one, will have a cost so high that you will pay for it, one way or another, forever and with the additional trauma of blood, sweat, and tears. It will be the most expensive fifteen minutes of passion you can ever have. This is only stated if you don't want the loss. In the event you are looking for the Big D, by all means, but get ready for the expense and the large legal bills and should this spawn litigation, please call my law firm for representation.

> *I was having a really difficult financial year. I asked my wife what she would like for the holidays, praying that she would keep her requests to a minimum, as she knew the difficulties I was having. She said, "A divorce!"*
>
> *Well, that's Life, as I wasn't planning on spending that much!*

Larry the Cable Guy

◦⁀◦⁀◦

Chapter 19

◦⁀◦⁀◦

ONE STEP AT A TIME

Have you heard people say that you must build your life one brick at a time? Well, bullshit. Your life isn't that solid. Life is moving you around as you roll the dice or draw from its stacked deck of cards. At least for me, just when I believe that I am gaining solid ground, *wham*, Life throws me a hurricane. The bitch of it is that Life waits until I have just made a material change or put the new roof on the house before putting that hurricane on the horizon. It is almost as if I am better off doing nothing.

Maybe I should be less ambitious and desirous—keep my ambitions small and be disappointed less? Maybe that's not such a bad idea. With less ambition and smaller dreams, I might be able to actually sleep, as I will worry less about clients, overhead, payroll, taxes, new business, current business, and general expenses. Let the other guy build up his business, and I can capture his dreams when his hurricane washes ashore. I can work for him, simply doing my job, which I would do anyway and collect my paycheck without putting in my own investment or taking the risk. When the hurricane hits, I may lose a few days of work, but I won't lose any of my own investment. In fact, maybe I will get lucky as his investment blows into my yard and creates my own cheap opportunity. If he gets rich, good for him, as he took the risk. But for those riches and rewards, the businessman had to endure headaches, grief, sorrows, and troubles, and therefore, it is his just deserves, and I am happy for him and so should you be.

Be happy for those who endured and were brave enough to take risks and capture their dreams. These people, exercising their ambition, rose to the challenge and sought their goals. If people are not able to capture their goals or dreams, give them your condolences, as at least they tried. Meanwhile, they gave you a paycheck, and you should be thankful for that.

Do not begrudge a person for his or her successes. If you want what another person has, then step into the world and make it happen, independently, smartly, and for yourself. Don't look to take from others. Don't steal or capitalize off their trust in you. Don't blame them if they have more money than you do, and no, you are not entitled to their money. What you may not be aware of is that this entrepreneur's risks or accomplishments was greater than you knew and so too should be their reward.

The difficulties of life are proven over and over again by the dramas we all endure. Look at a child. A child is about smiles, fun, and happiness. Most children can find fun or something to play with anywhere. Now look at yourself. Where is that smile? At best, your smile is now a frown. A child's smile is ever present. A child smiles because life is simple and pleasurable. Children's difficulties come when you refuse to buy them the newest and latest Wii game or Apple something-of-another. You smile only because of *a* circumstance, *a* moment in time arising from *a* moment of pleasure. A child smiles as smiling is part of his or her life. Take a photo of yourself and your child. Your smile looks different from that of your child. Your smile is forced, crooked, and bitter. You shared the same day as your child; your child looks exactly like you, but not the smile. Your child, although sharing the same day, did not share the same concerns, thoughts, and pressures. Reality and its stresses are yours to bear, and the stresses you hide from your child are rewarded in his or her pretty and upturned smile.

Work Hard, for What?

Life cannot reward everyone at all times. We are taught that hard work will bring us just deserves. How many of you believe that these megastores, mostly giant retail chains ending with *mart*, are doing us good? You want to open your own business, you are willing to bust your ass by working hard, you are willing to lay it all on the line, but how, just how, can you compete with these giants that monopolize the manufacturers, the suppliers, the distribution and logistical channels, the mass marketing outlets, and whatever else you need to survive in today's consumer world. You cannot.

You may work harder, but the inherent disadvantages already facing you will prove all too powerful. In truth, your small business cannot compete against these monopolies no matter how hard you are willing to work. Your just deserves will not come, at least in the scope you're hoping for. The consumer only cares about his or her own wallet, not about your desire to become part of the illusion of some supposed "American dream." Suppliers will first provide the larger, more creditworthy chains with product and better pricing. Payment terms will be given to these box store chains, whereas your small business will have to pay COD. The truth is that competing in this world is extremely difficult given the inequities and favoritism. We will all wind up wearing Wal-Mart employee identification badges if things don't change. Again, just in case Obama is reading this book, *"Put liquidity back into the marketplace, intended for the working man, and watch the positive results that he or she does with it."* Banks must again loan, credit must again be given, and hard work must be rewarded. I believe American's want to work, want their *American Dream*, and want self-employment. *We the People*, again need access to the financial markets.

The only saving grace is that today's negative economy has changed the consumer—maybe not the consumer's wish lists but certainly the frequency and means by which he or she can consume. The Internet is also hurting these "mart" stores. Consumers, now buying online, are getting better prices and buying less. Discretionary spending is being clicked away. Less spending and less retail walk-in business hurts the bigger, more overhead laden "mart" stores, more so than it does the smaller competitor. I'm hoping that the game cards are swinging the pendulum back in favor of the small businessman.

Government, big business, and special interest groups chew us up every day and in every corner of the world. At some point, we must realize that we have all been deceived. I must be fair; big business is not in business to protect us. We should know that. Big business is for big profit and you would be naive or stupid to think otherwise. We have been conquered, and we didn't even realize we were at war.

Big government is more dangerous than big business. Big government is intrusive, costly, and a never-ending bureaucracy that the everyday person cannot battle; not even when correct. We cannot afford big government and cannot afford those that it supports. Sorry for the hard truth, but Life sucks. Now, get a job and stop living off the sweat of all the rest of us.

Our children do not need to purchase everything that big business sends to the markets or advertises as a *must have*. Crave a banana, not more clothes and jewels. Stop putting pressure on the breadwinners of the family. Every time you want something, stop and think about your craving. Is your craving an act of being spoiled? Do you want just because you have an itch to receive something new? Do you want just to be a pain in the ass? Do you want because you perceive receiving something as a measure of the giver's love? Do you want because of peer pressure or because the item is the "in thing" to have? Or do you want because you have a legitimate need and failing to have this item makes your life harder? Stop and think about your *wants and desires* and just how much pressure you put upon your father or mother or spouse or grandparents just to have something that you do not truly need.

In these financial times, if you are wanting with no legitimate need, then you are selfish and shame on you. Are you willing to give up something in order to receive what you are asking for? You must understand that you and your family have only a finite amount of discretionary money to spend and divide among the family, friends, and dog. Other people have needs as well; are you causing them to sacrifice their needs for you? Everyone needs to now chip in. Everyone needs to contribute to the family unit. Every child needs to actually begin to help at home and learn to save money for him or herself and the family. Every penny saved is a penny earned. If you want, then you need to help contribute. The world has changed. A family now needs many breadwinners; one alone cannot do it. There is no more American dream. We are watching the death of the American middle class, and unless and until our politicians figure out how to put liquidity and credit back into the marketplace, our middle class, our wallets, and our discretionary monies will continue to shrink.

Life starts some people on better board game spaces than it does others. Game spaces change; beware of a turn in your fortune. Take, for instance, the student who never goes out, studies with intensity, and gets picked on (bullied) by other children and, from time to time, stuffed into a locker. The child presses on as his parents insist that he will go to a great college, graduate school, and be rewarded with a dream job, while his tormentors grow older only to become his employees. This may or may not happen. I hope it does and I hope the hunted grow to become the hunters.

Life's injustices can also strip us of any just rewards. Certain children simply cannot compete with, cannot study for, and cannot prepare for some of Life's select perks offered to the privileged, such as family contacts, business connections, mannerisms, class status awareness and prejudice, commonalities, country club politics, personal appearances, family money, physical appearances, great physical bodies, girls with pretty smiles and big "boots" (of course)! The studying and the books didn't match up to these variables. The dream job went to someone else, not because of that person's intelligence, not because he or she studied and got great grades in school. His or her success had nothing to do with academic prowess or hard work, but rather with contacts, likeness, or looks, and all of your hard work and honor societies could not make a difference. So much for, no pain no gain.

Do not allow bitterness to consume you or my negativity to depress you. Revenge, too will only consume you and eventually ruin you. Revenge may have its time and place, but the costs will be very high. I cannot deny that vindication does taste sweet, but again, it is very expensive and time-consuming. The cost is probably greater than the reward and, like most attempts at justice, takes too long. Instead of revenge, your life and the quality of your living are better served should you move forward with positive energy. In truth, the best form of revenge is success in the faces of your foes.

Experience has taught me that what you feel—the aura you transmit—will be felt by others. If you desire shit, you will attract shit.

If you transmit happiness and possessiveness, you will attract the same. Misery loves company and attracts those similarly situated. Tomorrow will be a new day, and you must transmit possessiveness and success so as to attract the same. People want to be around winners. Don't waste your time or resources with negativity. Learn from past failures; don't foster their continuation.

$$\mathcal{C} \sim \mathfrak{D} \mathfrak{C} \sim \mathfrak{D}$$

Chapter 20

$$\mathcal{C} \sim \mathfrak{D} \mathfrak{C} \sim \mathfrak{D}$$

PRESUMPTIONS REGARDING LIFE

A presumption that the world around us is inherently good is naive, if not ignorant. Our mothers would have us all believe in such fairy tales as Santa Claus, the Easter Bunny, and the goodness of humankind. We soon start to wise up just trying to survive in our own school system. By junior high school, as we experience the meanness and cruelty of other children, we see the world for what it truly is. Life's apple pie contains rotten fruit.

No, Mom, the world around us and the people within it are not all good. The bad appear to be everywhere, and we have no escape from them. We must understand and be taught that there are different sides to the world around us and we must be prepared for them all.

Nothing Comes Easy

Nothing in Life comes or is supposed to be easy. Good fortune just doesn't fall from the sky. You must work hard, endure hardships, and go through various stresses in order to achieve. No pain, no gain and no shortcuts.

Let me share a story regarding Life and corner cutting. A person I had come to know began talking to me about purchasing a restaurant business, complete with ownership of the land and the accompanying parking lot. The business did have incredible potential, and the price being floated around was less than the market value of the raw real estate alone. From an investment perspective, it sounded like a good deal, providing that the property could be sold if the restaurant failed. I was still reluctant as I knew nothing about restaurants and was busy with my own full-time day job.

My buddy asked me how sure I was that I could negotiate a lower price, handle the legal work between the buyer and seller, and settle with the first mortgage holder on the restaurant and property. I said that I could. He told me that, if I was certain, then his friend would put up the purchase capital and we would each receive 25 percent of the stock in the business and real estate. This third-party friend of his, Manuel, would take 50 percent and primarily operate the business. He further represented Manuel as an experienced restaurateur who was looking to relocate but not change professions.

Later, Manny approached me, stating that he was looking to change his life and that this restaurant afforded him just the opportunity he was thinking about. He wanted to be a partner in this venture and said he would put up the purchase capital as well as all the restaurant knowledge and experience. He even told me that he had a restaurant on South Beach, Florida. I explained that I had a job, limited investment monies to put forth, and did not want to run or have any real involvement in a restaurant.

Months later, I began receiving communication from Manny that the business was not doing well. Manny began demanding more money from me. When I stopped giving him my hard earned money, he began blaming me for his wrongs and my lack of continued capital infusion. My 25 percent ownership began causing me a 100 percent headache.

The next thing I knew, Manny; our mutual friend; and their dirty, crooked lawyers made up a cause of action against me! Why me? Simple; I was the one perceived to have deep pockets as I worked for a living.

Skipping ahead to the lessons learned:

a. If it sounds too easy, it is. Separate your emotions from your commonsense judgment.

b. Don't ever rush into anything of importance. If a rush is required, don't do it. Opportunities are created not dropped from the sky. If you made your opportunity properly, then there would be no reason to rush.

c. Never go into business with people you do not know. What a large mistake I made. How stupid I was, as this lesson should have been common sense. Yeah, yeah, yeah, when I met Manny and our mutual friend, they seemed like such cool guys. I'm sure many people initially liked Ted Bundy as well.

Common sense should dictate that, if you don't know someone, you don't marry that person or become his or her partner. Get to know the other first—meet his or her family; attend mutual get-togethers in public places; share football games and beer-drinking binges; and watch, listen, and learn. Later, if warranted, build the relationship to a friendship.

If you are contemplating a business with a friend, don't cry if it fails. Accept the fact that most businesses and good ideas fail, and it was no one's fault. Especially with a friend, you must travel with your eyes open and only blame yourself when things don't turn out the way you wanted. If you are a control freak, then absolutely don't go into business or make an investment unless you are sufficiently involved and have sufficient precautionary controls in place.

d. Always enter a business relationship with legal and well-thought out contracts and supporting agreements. The devil is always in the details. If you write out the terms of your business deal, your clear intentions, and your understandings, then it is very difficult to later argue about them. If an argument is to be had, very often the written terms will clearly define a winner and an asshole. As an attorney, I will provide some free advice: Always, always, always provide your attorney with a draft or bullet list of your intentions, desires, wish lists, and items or points that you want to make, get across, and have everyone understand. Allowing your attorney to draft business contracts and agreements without the benefit of your intentions and notes and an explanation of the spirit of the business transaction will probably turn out shortsighted. You will get an agreement filled with legalese and one-sidedness as opposed to the parties' joint intent.

Going into business with another person(s) is like walking into a family. You must first take the time to make your lists, analyze your pros and cons, and know what it is you want. If you are not going to take the time to do things correctly from the beginning, then you shouldn't do the business to begin with. Your engagement with a future business partner should take longer to mature than your engagement with your lover.

Never take in partners who are not fully committed with something hard to lose. Don't partner up with people who are not putting into the business something "hard" and "tangible"— something they will lose if the business fails—such as money, assets, their life, or collateral. A party who has nothing to lose but his or her time should be made an employee—especially if this party is asking to receive financial compensation along the way and before you. My risk is to be my reward. Your paid time makes you an employee and does not give you any rights to further cause me greater risks or enhanced legal responsibilities.

e. Partners must each be able to handle the liabilities of the business. This applies to the ability to make good on their signature as well. For instance, your partner can sign with you for a bank loan. However, if he or she doesn't have the backing to support the note when it comes time to pay the bank back, the bank doesn't care from whom it gets paid. The bank merely wants to get paid and will wind up suing you both—individually. Your collection problem with your partner is your problem. Thus, at the day's end, it will be you paying the bank and salvaging the business. This other partner maintains the benefits of partner without really sacrificing anything, except possibly his or her credit, which must already be deficient if the partner was unable to hold up his or her financial end in the first place.

f. Never go into a business unless you have sufficient understanding of the business, sufficient protections and safeguards, and a comfortable level of control. I am not saying that being a silent partner is always a bad investment. If your contracts are correct, then you should be properly protected in the event of a legal claim. In systems that provide free access to the courthouse, even a proper contract will not prevent you from being sued, but it should at least allow you to sleep knowing that you have built some defenses.

You must have a high degree of trust or faith in others before you to get into bed and close your eyes, as they take control of the business and your investment. As long as you understand the gamble you are making, then I wish you the best of luck and see nothing wrong with your crap shot.

However, if the business does not make it, do not cry over spilled milk and do not blame anyone else for its failure or your loss. This is Life. You knew the risks, you did not want to handle or control the business, and you trusted the unknown. You gambled and lost, and that is that. This same concept applies to all circumstances you get yourself into on blind faith and blind trust. The same way you would have taken the credit for making money, man up and accept the losses and take responsibility for your actions, good or bad. Also, recognize that, should the gamble lose, it may not be anyone's fault. Most businesses or investments fail. If not, everyone would be wealthy.

Chapter 21

GRASS IS ALWAYS GREEN AND BROWN

Many of us do our best to move forward in Life without friction. However, Life has no fun if it cannot run interferences, bump us off the game board a few times, drop the dice on us, lose our get-out-of-jail-free card, and not allow us to pass "go." Life owes me two hundred dollars for the last time I circled the board, and I have no faith Life will pay me when I now pass "go" again.

For so long, I thought that Life just had it out for me. I'm happy to report that I was wrong. *Life has it out for us all*. We will all have our good times and our bad times, and if we live long enough, we shall see this pendulum swing back and forth several times.

Understanding that Life is not fair and will not reward us appropriately for our sacrifices, we should no longer dream of grand illusions, two and a half kids, a dog with no fleas, or white picket fences surrounding our new home. It is best to dream for less and protect yourself against further disappointment. You are not cheating your ambition; you are simply acknowledging the realities of Life and not setting yourself up for either disappointment or the takeaway. Treat Life as a vacation, which is a trip around Life's game board. The more you pack, the more you have to carry and be responsible for. This applies even to the puppy you want.

Carry much, worry about much, and suffer the weight. Do not think that others will help you schlep the load. What you bring is what you must be responsible for. Pack light, travel fast, worry about less, and navigate the game board much easier.

Age and wisdom teach us to travel Life's game board inconspicuously. It is the young, the egotistical, or the foolish who want to be seen. This becomes a hard and usually very costly lesson to learn, as it is human instinct to want to show off, brag, draw attention to oneself, and make oneself feel better at the expense of others. The happier you are about yourself, the less you need, the more positive you remain, and the more self-restraint you will have.

Life Is about Survival

The world around us is quickly going to hell. Our national debts are overwhelming; we have lost all our savings due to the greed of others who are supposed to be looking out for us; our safety and security are in jeopardy; our businesses are failing; there are no jobs for our children, our graduates, or our seniors; our world is melting and our waters rising; natural disasters are increasing, our governments cannot get a grip; people are going to become even more dangerous as their own desperation intensifies; and our cries of pain are going unanswered. It appears the only way to fix one problem is by creating another.

To make matters worse, our own government is treading on us. Our government blames others, creates laws against others, and uses the justice system to destroy others and us as collateral damage. But in truth, it is the government who deserve to be on trial. Our constitutional amendments are being voided, modified, edited, or ignored by those who are supposed to enforce them. With the world being more dangerous and our governments less able to protect us, we need our guns and ammo more than ever. Our government wants us to be fully reliant upon it for every aspect of life. This sucks, as "we the people" are blind to the fact that we have been conquered by our own government. We shouldn't be forced into blind reliance upon our government. Our government should provide us some necessary tools and social obligations, but it is our responsibility to get off our asses and make living happen for ourselves. Government should not micromanage us or our bedrooms, and we shouldn't rely upon the government for survival.

What is there to smile about? Everyone I talk to has money problems, job concerns, family troubles, the belief that he or she is undervalued and underappreciated, too much to do, and not enough time or resources to do it with. This is Life? What are we supposed to look forward to? A little good news might help. Nightmares are born from the world around us. The demons that haunt us are all present. If this is not your world, you must be one of the chosen few who happened to be born right, simply lucky, on a slow-moving pendulum or have enough money to buy your problems away.

We are still animals who happen to wear clothes and have material objects. The laws of nature still apply to humans. Some of us are predators, some of us are herbivores; some of us are docile, some of us are untamed; some of us are trained, and others operate using nothing more than their natural instincts. "Do you eat green eggs, Sam I am?" Together we compromise the total range of the animal kingdom. Life has given us an ego and clothing, but not without costs. So few within today's society know how to hunt, prepare food, build a shelter, create clothing, or grow agriculture. A country boy can survive.

Today's generation of children only knows how to bang away on a keyboard; their handwriting's deplorable, and without spell-check or a calculator, they are lost. Take away our children's electronics, and their world shatters. Remember the days when you were happy just to open and rip apart a box. Well, today's kids are not happy with the box; they want only what's inside that box, which better be expensive, fancy, brand-named, and next year's model. How wrong we have made the world.

Today's society causes us to suppress our true instincts until we finally burst from our primal essence. What happens to a monkey when it gets frustrated and antsy? The monkey will literally begin throwing its own shit. What then do we expect from humankind when we get frustrated and antsy? Why would we expect anything less? What winds up happening is that our society provides little release in order to dispel pent-up anxieties and frustrations, which will certainly boil over. The physicality of humankind has been wrongfully and regrettably suppressed.

It is not a matter of where we can release such anxieties or nervous energies but when. In the First World, the work expectations are so high, the financial pressures so great, and the competition so enormous that work also becomes a survival task. So our pressures increase and our ability to shed our stresses decreases. In the First World, we live to work, and our work becomes our task master.

We love our violent sports, our fast toys, our slutty women, our barroom brawls, and our competitions, as they provide us with needed frustration releases and testosterone boosts. We are controlled by so many rules, regulations, laws, lawyers, and big government that we don't even know what we can or cannot do anymore.

My wife and I developed a real estate project on the absolutely most gorgeous piece of property in Central America. We had allowed our full-time staff and workers to live on the property, in quaint yet modern cottages that we would later use for VIP guests. Every view overlooked the entire valley, directly out to the Pacific Ocean, complete with the most incredible sunsets. The stars were so close you felt as if you could jump directly into the Milky Way. Nature and wildlife were abundant, and every man and woman on this property was physically fit without even realizing it or trying to be. And, yes, you could take a leak anywhere you want; mark your territory and keep the wolves away.

Meanwhile my wife and I lived in the valley below. We busted our asses working within the retail segment of the local economy. We dreamed that, one day, we would be able to move onto our mountain property. Our financially less inclined employees lived where we only dreamed to live, and of course they wanted more.

We would spend our days and sometimes weekends up on our mountain, only to have to drive back down to the city, no matter what, on a Sunday evening. The drive to the mountain always seemed shorter than the ride back home.

We lived in the city because, for some reason, we believed that, until we could build a house fit for magazines, we should not move to the mountain. Shame on us for believing this way, as there is no failure in accepting limitations while still fulfilling dreams. So the house would be a little smaller, but it would be a home. So, it wouldn't be so fancy, but what a view. So, we wouldn't have a Mercedes, but we would have a ranch with real horsepower. So we wouldn't have so many people around us, but we wouldn't have the crime and traffic that comes with population. So our friends may live closer to the kids' school, but I bet it is our mountain their kids all want to come and play on. So the community wouldn't have a fancy guard, but we would have Smith & Wesson guarding us. A smaller home would have meant less for the kids to clean. And by the way, I feel much safer with my own Smith & Wesson and Remington protection than I do waiting for the police to maybe respond to a 911 call. In hindsight, I needed only to dream smarter and make our limitations work for us, instead of viewing our limitations as a handicap.

Chapter 22

So Little Control

I remember being completely trapped in my work week, which was every day. I longed to run away or take time off, but I feared doing so. Clients don't care about your needs or your personal issues. Clients are paying for you to be in your office 24-7 and perform miracles. Staff doesn't fill in the blanks when you are gone. Let's face it, when the cat is away, the mice will play. Competition has no loyalty and will quickly prey upon your clients while you are not watching the store. Just wait until they try to take a vacation; paybacks are a bitch.

It can take years to obtain certain clients but only moments to lose them. Your staff has no loyalty except to their paycheck. Some employees become nothing more than paid thieves. Protect your business from everyone, as tomorrow your staff and/or partners may betray your deepest secrets with only their intended benefits in mind.

Judgments

We are not born knowing "right" from "wrong." "Right" and "wrong" are learned judgments. We are born with our instinct to survive. Right and wrong sway and bend in deference to our need to survive. One man's wrong may be another man's right, depending upon the situation—just as one man's loss may be another man's gain.

I do believe that most of us would like to be morally correct. However, actions are dependent upon personal abilities, circumstances, and experiences. A kid in the street does not share the same charitable desires as the kid living in Trump Plaza. The man losing his business probably no longer can afford to see the moral highroad as being so black and white, especially when he has to support his family. The hungry lion will look to the skinny deer as a fine meal, whereas last month, the skinny deer may not have been worth the rundown if the lion had just eaten.

Have you ever thought about the correlation between today's violence and the suppression of our basic instincts? Today's civilized society has no place for us to play caveman. We, as a species, need the outdoors, a sense of freedom, the ability to run and jump, the feeling of conquest, the campaign of a good battle, and the fear of not knowing whether or not today is the day we will be eaten. Today's society has caged us. We live in houses with bars. We work in offices with small, confined walls. We spend hours a day driving in cars smaller than most cages. Even the best leather chair wears thin over time. We are forced to play Tarzan in a concrete jungle where we act out our basic primal instincts with clever intellectual maneuvers instead of physical exertion. I am sure that, within the next five hundred years, our species will lose many of yesterday's needed physical characteristics. No longer are these the days when men are real men, as our society and rules have tamed and regulated us.

We can no longer run, jump, conquer, engage in battle, protest, or act out. Even our children can no longer behave as children. We are scared to let our children outside to play. Can you imagine that? What a sick world. In fact, we no longer really have a place for children to play. All of our land, with the exception of a few parks, most without sufficient bathrooms, is taken or restricted. Our children are growing up resistant to outdoor activities and allergic to physical exercise. I do have such a park close to the house but cannot play there, as the municipality did not install bathrooms or any that work. If I did find a suitable tree by which to relieve myself (the only option the municipality has left me with) and I were to be caught doing so, I could be forever branded as a *sexual predator* under current laws. Can you imagine such a brand for watering a tree?

In today's environment, we prefer our children within the confines and safety of our homes, snuggled in the couch or in their room, equipped with all of the latest electronic gadgetry. Amazing how we pretend to keep our children safe indoors by giving them electronic games that come complete with more sex, drugs, and violence than the Vietnam War. Talk about dangerous ironies and Pandora's box. We are purchasing for them exactly what we want to protect them from. What a twist. So next time your kid tells you they know how to do something, please understand they do know, except only in their virtual world, which has no real consequences and no real-world experiences. Our children actually believe their virtual skills are good enough for the real world. Driving a car in your Wii game is *not* the same as driving on the streets of Miami. Children do not even recognize the consequences or gravity of their actions, as pain is not felt and the consequences of the games' actions are not truly experienced on the Xbox or PlayStation.

Children grow fat, lazy, and unskilled in reality, and weak within nature. We have lawyers fight our wrongs and use these lawyers and laws in improper ways so that we can weasel out of our own wrongdoings and escape our responsibilities. Someone should create a game in which the lawyers are the first to be eaten, and those who hired the lawyers to wrongfully assist their false efforts should be first beaten before being eaten.

As a species, we should be seeing more green and far less black from the tarmacs or white from the concrete. We should all begin our party where the blacktop ends. Our jungle should be natural, not made from glass, concrete, and steel. We would feel so much better if we could run with grass underneath our feet and feel the vastness of Mother Nature.

Today's society punishes our primal behavior. We were all born naked and free. Humanity was born without the aid of fire, wheels, clothing, retail shopping, and fast food. Later, humanity engaged in fighting grand battles; yielding heavy, sharp blades; and exploring the vast world. We nixed our pent-up energies by walking or farming and, on occasion, slicing and dicing a rival tribe. Now we ride in the backseats of limos and can only release our anxieties by pushing paper and lifting files. When we do seek to reach into ourselves, we are punished by—what else—jail and more cages.

We must find a way to be men again, men and women as we once were, and safely roam the planes grunting and grinding—not full time, not as a digression in evolution, but as a means of play and exercise. We must play, with a little danger and risk, so as to feel the adrenaline pumping.

There is a lot of truth to men needing to be men and boys needing to be boys. We have substituted our horse for man-made horsepower, and then—would you believe it?—we even curbed how fast we are allowed to gallop. We have substituted the use of the sword for the pen. We go to the latte club instead of the fight club. We have substituted our craving for the hunt for McDonald's Happy Meals and now even attempt to dictate how large of a cup we can drink from. All of these docile substitutions cannot be good for us as a species. Repressed basic, primal needs will surface, and when they do, watch out. You may resort to writing a horrible book and calling it *I Don't Care What Mom Says, "Life Sucks."*

I am not advocating for a rougher, tougher, lawlessness; well, maybe a little vigilante should be permissible. I am advocating for a society that allows for some unleashed aggression in a safe manner. Our society places too much emphasis on corporate warfare, the need to make lots of money, and the desire to spend this money faster than we make it. We need to change our belief and structure modality so that we are finding ways to free ourselves and not enslaving ourselves to our careers. Life is strangling us, changing us; we need to push back to nature, back to our essence.

Toughen Up

We no longer take responsibility for our actions, as we have forgotten how to "man up" or "toughen up." Today's society looks to shed blame, as blaming others is a lot easier than taking the responsibility for our own actions or inactions. This is an enormous societal issue that we are not addressing. Frivolous claims and cries of wolf should be met with serious consequences. People who refuse or fail to take responsibility for their own improper actions or wrongdoings must be taught that such conduct is unacceptable. If these same people intend to cause grief, harm, and injustice upon others for their own failures, stupidity, or entitlement belief, then these people should be met with commensurate punishment.

Don't tattletale and don't blame others. Toughen up. This concept is lost on us, as our new way of life has us working alone from behind a computer screen. Today's society no longer works well with others. This society no longer recognizes concepts such as *honor among thieves* or *take responsibility for yourself or others if you are their leader* or *don't do the crime if you don't want to do the time.*

I have personally watched children conduct improper actions, and when their parents say, "Who did it?" the child responds, "It wasn't me," or, "My brother did it." Sometimes the child says it so cute that he or she actually gets rewarded by laughter or smiles instead of punished. We are fostering this incorrect behavior.

Injustice

As an attorney, I witness people conspiring against others as the not-so-just system encourages them. The Dark Side needs no practice or enticements to lie, cheat, swindle, hustle, and steal. Our system of justice gives everyone an audience without the need or necessity to first submit sufficient proof of his or her claim. All that is required is the mere filing of a legal document called a "complaint." Then, wham, you are in court and the accused must go through a long, lengthy, tiring, stressful, and expensive process merely to prove his or her innocence. In spite of what you have read about our system of justice, we are all guilty until proven innocent, and we are all innocent until we run out of money. Most falsely accused people wind up paying some form of legal extortion just to get out of the drama. The bad guys and their shyster lawyers know it. We need a new Lady Justice and, this time, one who is not blind.

In our "justice" system, there is always lying. There are so few honest people, especially given what is at stake. If the claimant's case is grounded in oral testimony, then we should raise the evidentiary bar so as not to reward the best liars. This will force people to use more objective measures in the future and take better care of their affairs.

Responsibility should be rewarded and stupidity shunned. We should not leave everything to fate or the decisions of others.

If the defendant is guilty, then so be it. However, in my long and consuming career, I have seen more than my fair share of lying plaintiffs motivated by money, greed, revenge, retaliation, mischief, selfishness, or whatever else you can imagine to score an undeserved victory. I even saw a case where the claimant was trying to have my client thrown in jail just because the claimant was in love with my client's wife and believed that, if my client went to jail, then he would be able to get to my client's wife. I have seen ex-spouses or ex-business partners create horrible fictions against the other merely for spiteful and malicious purposes. These people have no conscience and must not have had a mother, as the truth of the facts asserted vanishes from the equation.

No wonder no one wants to admit wrongdoing! Lady Justice is not only blind but corrupt and susceptible to biased pressures. The legal system, different than a justice system, works best for the wrongdoers, liars, extortionists, blackmailers, the wealthy, criminals, and the insane. So what does this have to do with Life? Everything; this is the game we must play and the board we must play upon. This so-called legal system makes and enforces the rules making *The Days of Our Lives* always a drama, horror, and trauma. Don't tread on me!

Chapter 23

Life Has Taken Our Children

Many of our problems begin with our children—how we raise them; how they perceive the world; and, very importantly, how they interact or survive. With each generation, Life has become harder and harder to survive. Life now provides much more competition and, thus, fiercer battlefronts. Life is now playing us globally. We are no longer competing only with our classmates but with the world's classmates. Languages, cultures, ways and means, logics, and viewpoints are all different and those willing to learn them create their opportunities. Even the weather is now a global threat.

In today's era, children are lost in spite of being connected. Children know of only instant messaging, cellular phone functions, and e-mailing. Well, I'm sorry, but those were not the skill sets or job qualifications that I was hoping my kids would dazzle the business world with.

Life Shakes up the World Leaders, Not Just You and Me

The world and its governments must play on Life's game board along with the rest of us. With each roll of Life's dice and change of game board positioning, Life causes shifts in power, economy, and circumstances. Due to the size of countries' governments, Life's changes may take longer to feel, but it happens. For instance, look at education. The

United States has fallen from number one to number twenty-four in the world. The US will lose intellect, jobs, technology, and much more to children from other countries in the fields of engineering, computer hardware development, computer software development, medicine, science, biology, alternative energy development and deployment, robotics, and banking. While our children play with their Game Boys, fixed on the couch, other children from around the globe are thinking about their grades and how they will be competing in tomorrow's global markets. Come on, parents, wake up and get your kids' priorities back on course.

Today's children simply expect to be handed the world and everything within it. We have unjustly spoiled them and encouraged their fantasy world. Life will not be as nice to our kids as their parents have been. Life will unmercifully crucify our children when they bring their spoiled act and tantrums to the real-world circuit. Our children must understand that everything, and I mean everything, must be earned. Our children must understand that they must affirmatively take actions that make people like them, want to be with them, and respect them. People don't like people simply because; only your mommy will love you that much.

In order for children to be liked, they must know how to please, know how to behave, how to be liked, how to be polite, and how to appreciate what and who are around them. Children must learn how to share. Children must learn how to talk to others and socialize. This cannot be done when children are hooked on antisocial technology.

If government is advocating taking away my guns and ammo, before doing so, it should take away both tobacco and the electronic idiot boxes everyone's kids are now addicted to. Don't take away my play toys when you are allowing children to play with games that promote and are more violent than my range shooting. Gun ranges do not allow smoking, alcohol, or these idiot boxes inside their facilities. Guns don't account for forty percent of every Medicare dollar spent as tobacco does.

Chapter 24

DISAPPOINTMENTS

L ife is hard and full of disappointments, dangers, and stress. Children must be prepared for reality. My mother tells me that children should not have to be subjected to such harshness, as they are just children. I disagree. I am not saying that you should take away their childhood and rose gardens, but I am saying that we must leave the thorns on the stems so the children handling them learn to beware of the pricks. Teach your children reality and how to recognize and handle pricks, and allow them to walk the game board with less stress and more comfort.

Life is not about "give me," "get me," and "buy me." Children must learn that Life does not center on them; in fact, Life controls them. They cannot demand as they do. Children must learn and be made to understand why certain bad things are happening to them and to others, why good guys finish last, and why the hero dies in real life. If we don't explain to them that this is how Life really is, then children will be forever dazed, confused, and depressed.

Life is about *good versus bad*, and many times, knowing just what is black and white may be difficult. Black and white often don't truly exist—replaced instead by the sundry and subjective shades of gray. And furthermore, you may believe you're operating within the gray, only to find that another person sees the situation as black and white, therefore holding you responsible. Bad things happen to good people, and injustices occur. Children must be taught to handle these pressures, stresses, and anxieties. If not, our poor children will not be able to cope. Crying only helps to release the emotions; it does not solve the issues. In fact, crying may exasperate the problem, as crying is not a solution but a reaction.

How can we expect our children to help us? How can we expect them to handle the world and to become masters or leaders of their futures and that of others? How can we expect our children to appreciate our parental sacrifices and our own needs if we don't educate them about the world they will have to live in without our protection?

I remember how long it took me to finally understand and cope with the fact that Life has different rules for different people. As a child, I would drive myself crazy not understanding why someone could do something and get away with it while I could not. Mom led me to believe in the fiction of equality. Well, boys and girls, Life is not equal. For all the wrong and unfair reasons, some fortunate people simply will not be adversely affected by their actions or inactions like the rest of us. It sucks, yes, but that is Life.

From a parent's perspective, we have to deal with our lives, our children's lives, our family unit, and the world around us. We have life pressures, daily pressures, family pressures, partner pressures, sexual pressures, job pressures, business pressures, lots and lots of financial pressures, and pressures regarding our children, which seem to outweigh them all, and then we have our pressures on top of our pressures. It's got to be my buddy, Matt's, fault. Some buddy! Children should be shown the pressures that their family faces, not shielded from them. I'm not advocating that our children should be faced with fixing the family unit, but they should at least understand the realities of it so that maybe they will become part of the solution.

Maturity and growing up know no age. While it is not our place as adults to use our children as sounding boards or look to them for answers concerning adult problems, children must know when to at least back off, stop wanting, when to ease our adult pressures in simple yet thoughtful ways such as by performing chores, household work, doing well in school, appreciation, manners, politeness, remaining quiet, saving money, and staying out of trouble.

How dare society's moral hypocrites challenge parenting discipline when they allow television shows and video games full of sex, violence, and wrongdoing, which influence our kids right before our eyes? Children cannot escape the immoral and illegal behaviors that are being thrust upon them; hell, Congress streams their hearings right into our living rooms; now that is scary.

By no means am I advocating for a sterile environment and do like a good T 'n' A show myself, but come on, have you seen what these kids are looking at? I can't believe *Hustler* and *Penthouse* magazines are under attack by any group when I see the craziness that is being beamed by the Internet directly to our children—the same Internet and games we are purchasing for our kids. Video games are teaching our children how to hijack cars, rob old ladies, and brutally kick the shit out of anyone walking down the street. In fact, today's games and television are encouraging and enticing our inner primal instincts. If these kids are not taught wisely, they will act upon their primal behavior in real life and face real consequences. Can it be that we are actually grooming criminal behavior as part of today's norm? Mom wants to know how this can happen. The world eventually sneaks into the shelter Mom built. It sneaks in through the very electronic toy keeping the kids quiet while mom is busy in the shelter! What these kids must learn is that, when you get punched, it hurts. *Virtual reality is not reality.* Kids say they understand this distinction, but I'm not convinced. I'm not convinced, as kids today, for the most part, only know of virtual reality and, therefore, have little to compare it to.

Many of us live relatively sheltered existences. The vast majority of the world is financially impoverished. Thus, how do you think children from these walks of life see the world? How do you think these parents view the world? Those individuals who clean the toilet bowls of others and put up with their spoiled, snot-ragged kids must see the world in a very pessimistic light. Consider the family that has spent every last cent it had and could borrow in order to get their child medical treatment; just how do you think they view living? *You want a Reality Show. Watch Life.*

Life Is Controlling Us, But Are Our Children the Boss?

When and where did Life change the game board positions allowing the balance of power between child and parent to switch? Our spoiled children know that this transference of power has occurred. In school they are taught about their rights, child abuse, 9-1-1, and God and encouraged to report their parents if they feel their parents have wronged them. I have heard kids tell their parents, "I am the boss of myself," or say things like, "You didn't make me. God did," or even suggest that, if their parents threaten them, they will call 9-1-1.

Parents have gotten accustomed to hearing their children rant, rage, and tantrum, and we give in to these behaviors. Children demand and exert independence and authority as if they knew what that was. Worst of all, given our busy and hectic days, we let our kids utter such demands or exhibit negative behaviors because we don't want to directly deal with this misconduct at that moment. Life has tired us out and worn us down, and we just want some peace and relaxation. So, heck, it is easier to buy them their own television so that we can watch our old one without hearing their nagging. Wrong. Children were made by us and for us. Children must know that their parents are to come first and that they must respect us and adhere to our wishes. Children will one day become adults and understand exactly what I am talking about and wish this type of behavioral modifications from their own kids. It is our TV, not theirs. We are the boss, not them. If they don't learn by being instructed, by being structured, then discipline is warranted. Why is a spanking now illegal or scorned? If your son does not learn to fear his mother when he is young, he certainly will not fear her when he is taller than she is. Then what is Mom to do? No, I'm not advocating a beating. I said spanking. A spanking is a disciplinary measure, meant more to scare and certainly not to cause real injury. I just want to clarify my point, as I'm sure my mother doesn't approve of my advocacy.

If your child doesn't like what you want to watch on your older TV, he or she can read a book or study for the SATs. Do not purchase your kids their own flat screen merely to shut them up. You have taught the baby well. The more he or she cries, the more he or she will get. Dumbass, you are being controlled.

Life has allowed the pendulum of extremes to swing against us. Children were originally meant to help their parents, to listen to their parents' age-earned wisdom, to be disciplined when need be, and to respect their elders. We had large families to help tend to our businesses or farmwork. Children were in school or in the fields or both. Regardless, they didn't sass their mommas, and they did what they were told. Today, we may be the parents, but we're certainly not the boss. Stupid us. Life has led us so astray, and not only do we see it and talk about it, we appear helpless to the situation. Amazing and let me say again, stupid us. But hey, that's Life.

Time to Take a Break

It is 1:30 a.m., and I'm tired. We just finished summer vacation, and I have driven a thousand miles listening to my four children rant while doing everything I could in order to provide them with positive memories and a great time to take back to school and share with their friends. I have tried to please everyone and have taken them on a countrywide trip so they could see, learn, have fun, and experience as much as possible during this summer vacation. Not even a thank you. Thanks, Life.

Children are ignorant to the fact that you too are human and have feelings and needs. My chest pains worsen each day. While my attacks used to scare me, I now smile during the pain. I am fully aware that only two things can happen; either Life will finally allow me to go in peace or Life will not allow me to go, and therefore, why worry? In any event, do you think the kids notice when I'm hurting? Not a chance; and if they do notice, apparently they don't give a shit.

Anyway, an hour ago, just before I came upstairs to write and calm down, my daughter woke my wife and myself up because she couldn't sleep. She woke, not from a nightmare or a loud noise. No, this was simply a case of "I'm up, so what are you going to do about it?" You know, "Entertain me." She is almost fourteen but had to wake us up so that I could get her back to bed. And in return . . . well, I'm up and of course my wife is rightfully pissed, but at me! Yeah, Life again.

The night before, my nine-year-old son did the same thing. He went to the bathroom in the middle of the night, turning on every light in the house, making all kinds of noises, and then having a casual conversation with the dog, who is loud on her own. Then he went to bed as if nothing had happened, leaving the dog still thinking it was playtime and leaving my wife and me tossing and turning for an hour trying to get back to sleep. Thanks again, Life.

Chapter 25

YOU GOT JACKED

You finally meet that special someone in your Life. You date, get to know each other, have great multi-daily sex, and talk about marriage. Many women start to think about a family and what their children will look like with their new man. Like grows into love, and eventually, love blossoms into marriage. There are lots of scenarios that can lead people or force people to the point of marriage—shotgun wedding, baby on the way, drunk in Vegas, immigration, sex, your only sex—but eventually we get there.

The story continues . . .

For the majority of people, we begin our marriage young and broke but in love and having sex. There is still that sweet, innocent talk about children and how happy kids will make us; did I say that we are having lots of sex? For others, marriage begins to fade, leaving these troubled couples having discussions about starting a family in the hopes that a new bundle of joy will reignite their marital flame. Then there are those who just believe they are ready to begin their marriage, as they wear a sex smile. Dumbass, that is going to be expensive and life-changing sex. Women, please, smarten up. Your man really doesn't want to start a family; he wants sex. You are talking about babies, and he is only thinking about what it takes to make them. The decision to have kids and when to have kids is controlled more by the woman, as the man's brains and reasoning no longer exist once his little head begins the thinking. Women, we men really—and I mean really—are that stupid once our little head takes over. This is not an excuse but a preemptive apology, and you will need to think for the both of us.

Anyway, you get pregnant. Your families are happy and sharing the gossip. E-mails, parties, and closeness are abounding with love, joy, and excitement. Life is changing around you, all because of this creation. It appears that having a baby was a good idea after all. Just wait.

Life begins to change—for you and your partnership—as your wife begins to show. Now you spend your money on the baby's room instead of alcohol-induced weekends in Cancun. You spend your time speaking about baby names instead of having adult conversations. Wild sex and parties craved by the young and fearless are no longer in your vocabulary, as you have now turned into serious parents-to-be. Your wife now begins to complain about things you've never heard before. Hormones are flooding your home; only for you, they smell like sex, and for her, well . . . let's just say you aren't getting any tonight.

Yes, in a short period of time, you went from having the lifestyle of the young and restless to living the lifestyle of those growing up too fast. Your bride is now showing, which is of, course, spooking you. You, being in your early twenties and hanging around other girls with their young twenty-year-old bodies, are getting your first heavy dose of temptation. Hang on, buddy. Be fair to your young bride; she's having your child. You and your little friend put that child there. I know, now you understand the importance of birth control. The pregnancy is causing a whirlwind of emotions and personality changes that your youth is just not prepared for or mature enough to really handle. Love becomes . . . well, it becomes simply marriage now with a kid on the way. Everything that you had once thought about doing, spending money on, or getting crazy about, including ways in which you were going to have "monkey sex," is suddenly out of the picture. But hey, the family is soooo excited! Lucky you and just wait!

Let's just recap for the moment. You were young and had life by its balls. Things were really looking up, as you were in love; were a gorgeous couple; and had all the things that youth brings, including a great body, beautiful looks, plenty of hair, energy, a small refrigerator by your bed full of vodka and Red Bull, an un-shattered vision of the world, ambition, and dreams. Now you are married, pregnant, and emotional. Life is changing and not all of these changes are for the perceived better—not exactly what you bargained for. Certain dreams are already getting shattered; for the first time, you are having couple fights; your fast-paced, anything-goes lifestyle is now fraught with responsibility, lack of fun, and lack of alcohol; and you had to switch to decaf lattes. Your friends are all jet setting and completely carefree. But hey, they don't know what they are missing with the joy of all this baby stuff.

Then it is time. People will argue as to what finally brings about the birth. Some say it is a big meal; others say it was the walk around the park, the full moon, indigestion, or drama. Or maybe it was because you finally got laid again. I believe that the water finally breaks because the body must divert some of that fluid away from your tear ducts. I found that labor usually happens shortly after some type of family and friend get-together; usually someone's mother does something to boil the pot over.

Here you are at this shindig. You are pregnant and looking like an explosion about to happen, your emotions are highly volatile, you and your husband have been having some inner challenges, and you are prohibited from alcohol. This absence of liquor has taken its toll on you, and tonight is no exception. At this shindig, you are hearing great stories from tanned friends and family who just got back from exotic travels, and your husband's best friend is showing him that new sports car that he just bought—the one your husband had always wanted, had dreamed of having before the rest of his friends, and can now no longer have. But hey, minivans now come with satellite radio and stylish rims. You are now sick of hearing about the anticipated baby, but the lectures on how to be a great parent continue. You selected a baby name nine months ago, but of course, there are always those wiseasses who want you to change the name. Both you and your husband are looking to bolt; if only you could have a few shots of tequila! Now that is a worthy name—"Tequila." Maybe for your next! Finally you must leave, as your back hurts, and you are cramping and experiencing lots of discomfort.

The car ride home is full of fun. Your husband is in one of those bitching moods, and all you want to do is get into bed. You bitch back, as, after all, your husband isn't pregnant; what is he so pissed about? Home, finally. You think silently that there's not a chance your husband will be getting laid tonight.

You get tucked into bed. You are as comfortable as it is going to get. Your husband takes a nightcap so as to ignore his penis, which desperately wants your attention. Later as both of you are in bed discussing the night's events and tragedies and dozing off, holy shit. Finally, you're in real labor. Shit, another sleepless night, and the bed is wet.

Men, now it is your turn to take over the work. Men, now you need to run like crazy and grab that emergency bag packed eight months ago. You call the doctor's answering service, put your wife into the car, and call your family and hers.

When my first child was born, my ex-wife was late in getting her epidural. The doctor had me bend over so that she could rest on my back while he was applying the injections. Leaning over on top of me—yeah that's what we will call it; it was more like trying to drive me into the floor, while the doctor was sticking her with a needle the size of her arm. Well, she applied force, weight, and all of the unleashed hell she could muster, as only a pissed-off, pregnant woman could do, upon my back. After the doctor finished with the injections and the nurses had her comfortable, I fell to the floor in agony. Two years earlier, I had herniated a disc in my lower back. Her rage had just aggravated and exacerbated the injury that I was trying to keep away. So much for nursing an old wound. I literally crawled out of the delivery room, where my parents were waiting outside, along with some other friends and family members, who were all at this shindig and probably the root of tonight's fun.

My father, who is a doctor, recognized that I was in pain and ran to pick my sprawling ass up. While my ex-wife was now up, talking on the phone to her mother, who didn't bother to show up at the hospital, I was popping pain pills and waiting to see an orthopedic specialist who'd been paged from the hospital's emergency room. That evening, I was blessed not only with a baby girl but an MRI and trigger point injections. Yeah me!

Anyway, now you are at home with your family. Everyone is wall-to-wall smiles. The first few days are easy, as family stays to help. However, the company soon grows old, and people leave and allow you to act as the responsible young adults you are. You are parents. Wow, does that reality hit you. Life so far is batting fifty-fifty.

Now your bundle of joy is growing. Everything that you once thought was sacred, like your beer mug or music collection, is now trashed. Your creation is getting more active, and with each footstep you are losing memorabilia. Your past is being lost to your future at a rate now commensurate to your hair loss. "Can't you push this kid back in? Crawl again, damn it!"

In college I began collecting stereo equipment. By the time my first child was walking, my stereo equipment and speaker system were toast. My darling daughter literally brought the house down. It seems as if, one day, she went from crawling by to walking by the wall unit that housed my stereo components to climbing through it. Her athleticism started when she was really young. I remember the day. I watched as if it were happening in slow motion. My daughter went up, and the components came down. My stereo had survived wild college nights, law school, and move after move, but Life would not allow these components to survive a two-year-old. I was just so happy she was okay, and heck, she was so gorgeous. How could I possibly get angry at her? Besides, it had to be her mother's fault! Kidding.

I love watching the evolution of parents and child. With the first child, life becomes sterile. With the second child, a little dirt on the fallen pacifier can be overlooked. By the time the third child arrives, poor bugger, he gets a used pacifier.

Chapter 26

PLAYING WITH
TUNNEL VISION

My mother, for instance, and possibly yours, lives in what I would call a bubble. Although I understand my mom's way of protectionist thinking, I don't necessarily agree with it. I was my mom's firstborn and was the one responsible for all of her early and continued aggravation and heartaches. By the time my brothers came along, she had already been there, done that. I seasoned her as a parent. I was the learning curve. Did my brothers ever thank me? Of course not, but that's Life. My brothers only sought to rat me out whenever the opportunity arose. Did I ever help their cause!

Does your mom have too much free time? Free time is a danger. It means too much time to formulate unfounded opinions, too much time to take conjecture and turn it into *opinionated fact*, too much time to read the supermarket's trash magazines, and too much time to parrot innuendo. As a defense lawyer, any and all unfounded and objectively baseless allegations and accusations against someone else really burns me up. Why is it that those with the least amount of knowledge are always the ones to judge and offer their opinions the loudest? Reality check; gossip is not fact. In fact, I believe that tabloid magazines and daytime TV shows are more dangerous than guns. Why don't we ban these media trash mediums?

What we hear in the media is questionable, sensational, told to stimulate gossip and sales or ratings, and truthfully irrelevant. What we think we know, we don't. The truth is that 90 percent of what we hear, think we know, or listen to is bullshit. The media is the greatest of all the gossipers and illusionists. The media is a business that needs to sell and draw attention. The media must plan, extrapolate, elaborate, embellish, falsify, and do what any other business needs to do in order to sell, sell, and sell more. Today, the media is all owned by corporate giants who own lots of other businesses that, of course, utilize their parent media components and media divisions. Only you, the consumer, are probably not aware of the link between these business conglomerates and their need to exploit for profit. You don't actually believe that the news is fair, do you? The conflict of interest is well hidden amongst these shell companies and vertically integrated corporations, but it is there. The media makes kings and presidents who themselves are not even capable of challenging their creators.

I have arguments with such opinionated folks all of the time. I was on an Internet radio talk show that aired globally each evening. The guys and I brought up global, controversial issues that got addressed on a grassroots level around the world through the Internet on talk radio. When the O. J. Simpson case went to trial in Las Vegas, in September 2008, we started covering and discussing the case on air. I knew a lot about O. J., as I had represented him for a decade and one of my cohosts was O. J.'s good friend and promoter, Mark Norman Pardo. The show gathered a large, diverse, and heated audience. We had thousands of people listening to us each night. The comments concerning O. J. Simpson became very "colorful."

Our Internet talk show began fielding phone calls and chat room messages from what we dubbed the "House Mom Congregation." These mothers had all kinds of negative and hostile things to say about O. J. and wanted their perceived justice to be taken out through this completely separate, thirteen-year-later trial in Nevada. It appeared the audience wanted a man tried and convicted based upon a case already tried and a charge for which the accused was already acquitted. They wanted a hanging. They wanted the laws of our country broken in order to carry out what they perceived to be late justice. Now, I ask you, who is the criminal?

During these chats and calls, our team asked these house moms for the basis of their hostilities and opinions. *All*, and I mean *all*, of these separate individuals stated that they formulated their opinions about the LA murder case based on the limited amount of information they'd gathered while watching, from time to time, the O. J. case on TV, as well as being influenced by the media and tabloids after O. J.'s acquittal.

Now, I bring this all up to make the following point: Life sucks. The creation of rumors, gossip, and lies is just wrong, especially when it can cause so much damage to someone. You can basically accuse anyone of anything, and that poor schlep now has to defend him or herself against a lie. Defending a lie can be one of the hardest defenses ever. For instance, I can tell your wife that I saw you with a stripper in a hotel when in fact you were playing poker with your buddies—the same poker game that your wife had earlier said you couldn't go to, and therefore, you had told her you were working late. You are now stuck between some big lies and are going to get shit no matter what. The bottom line is that you are now in lots of trouble. It gets better, as I can tell this lie to your wife in such a way that her friends overhear it. The lie then spreads through rumor and gossip mills, and soon the entire community thinks you are a cheating piece of shit. Soon, your friends abandon you, as per their wives' instructions, your wife is embarrassed and angry, you are given dirty looks at your son's soccer games, and you have to hire a lawyer, all because of someone's viciousness against you.

In the end, after you smooth things out and dispel the lie, there is little to nothing you can legally do to the asshole who caused and disseminated the lie. Yes, you can sue, but doing so will be expensive and you still don't have a sure win, as the outcome will come down to he-said/she-said type of proof. If your wife first believed the lie, then isn't it possible that a jury might as well? All this aggravation and trouble because Life needed some extra entertainment.

Oops

Let me tell you a funny yet horrible real story that I bore witness to and was maybe part to blame for, as I was there. My wife, myself, and another couple took a weekend trip to the Bahamas. It was a spontaneous trip decided upon the day before and required only Brazilian bikinis and one toothbrush. The four of us brought so little that we all shared the same carry-on bag. The plane was delayed at Miami International Airport, and the girls started showing each other their sexy bikinis. They even went shopping in the airport for more of the lesser stuff!

My wife threw some of her sexy wear into the black bag, and away we later went. My wife is five foot six with lots of leg and, at 110 pounds, a size 0. She fits into the sexiest linens sold by Playboy or Victoria's Secret.

Well, to the Bahamas we went. When we arrived, we noticed that the clothes my wife had thrown back into the bag were not there. After the group recounted the events, we laughed as we realized that my wife had thrown these sexy pieces of floss into a similar black bag belonging to the gentleman who was next to us by the bathrooms. Now this poor schlep will have to explain the *dental floss* within his bag when his wife finds them. This poor guy has no idea and no reasonable explanation; he is completely innocent, but how does he explain what is in his bag?

As punishment for my wife, I kept her naked all weekend. "Bad girl."

Chapter 27

EVERYONE HAS
A DIFFERENT TAKE

Everything in Life has a cost and you either pay the price now or later, but you pay. I don't care what Mom says; you need money or like value in order to survive. Yeah, yeah, yeah, you can live low and live on love, but condoms and alcohol still cost money.

It takes lots of Life's experiences to teach you to look at issues from multiple perspectives simultaneously. Learning different perspectives is incredibly helpful in trying to better understand situations, events, and people's reasoning or mind-sets. Remember, be humble. Your way, your logic is not the only way or logic. I'm not saying that your way may not be more efficient or effective, but if the other person's alternative thinking takes him or her to the same place as yours, then there is really no reason for you to get crazy. Allow other people to travel their own roads, and you travel yours. If you say nothing, you won't be embarrassed if by chance they get to the finish line before you. What is important is that at the end of each road there is a bar in the middle that you can each raise a glass within.

Is the Grass Really Greener?

Life gives us the ill-fated concept of greener grass in order for us to trip all over ourselves while looking. The grass is not greener; it is only perceived as such. You must remember that grass is green, but the shades of green depend upon the variety of grass, the watering schedule for the grass, and the position of the sun. While you're walking through the grass—it does not matter who the grass belongs to or which shade of green it—watch out for the dog doo-doo.

Life is such a bitch that it won't let us enjoy our own field of grass. Once on our grass, Life has us automatically checking out the neighbors'. This act demonstrates our continuous need to need, be ridden with envy, or conquest. We can't just be happy with or recognize the enormous value of what we already have. As a species, we always want more and seem to have a problem narrowing our line of vision. Remember, there is no end to nice. Learn to be happy with what you have and only replace what you have when it breaks or no longer suffices.

Life's Dark Forces

We all know that there are bad people out there. The wrongful actions of these bad people infect decent people and cause them to do things they perhaps would not have otherwise thought of or done. Let me use a hypothetical to explain. You are a successful businessman and have a big and growing business. Life throws you a curveball. Life, just today, caused you to lose your biggest contract client. You have no idea why, but it happened. Next you hear that more of your clients are leaving you for the competition. You scramble. You lower your rates in order to keep clients. The problem is that your overhead is predicated upon your old, higher rates. Now, with lower rates, less clients and no growth, your overhead is choking you. You start to stumble both corporately and personally. Your stress, chest pain, and breathing problems are growing. Life's Dark Forces smell your stress and start to circle you. At the local watering hole, an old acquaintance bumps into you. This old acquaintance informs you that he has an easy way for you to make money. He tells you that he has a way for you to score some big and fast money.

A month or two ago, you wouldn't have said anything to this old acquaintance other than, "Hello, nice seeing you again." Today, you are discussing business, which smells a little funny, but you suppress your better judgment. Desperate times, at least desperate by your standards, have led you into a place that you would not have otherwise ever thought of or entertained. You are now contemplating taking action that you know or kind of know you shouldn't be thinking about. Poor judgment gets the best of you, as bankruptcy looms. You are not a bad person, just a desperate person.

The system then severely punishes you. Life bites. Life unfairly castrates you, as truly you are not a criminal, but acting as a father, a husband, the breadwinner of the family; you were thinking about feeding your family over and above everything else. Your sense of survival took over your judgment. Okay, you made a mistake. But for your survival instinct, you would never have contemplated doing what you did, which in perspective wasn't so horrible. Law enforcement issues encompass you, and now you again need lots of money, not only to cover your expenses but now to hire a legal defense team. To make matters worse, you lose your business anyway; six months from now you'll lose your defense lawyer because you can't afford him either, and your life will have gone from bankruptcy being your worst-case scenario to five years in prison and a family that will not be able to support itself. Life sucks.

False Judgments

We have no right to judge others, especially if we are missing pieces of the story, do not have firsthand knowledge, and do not know or are unwilling to listen to the complete set of proven or provable facts. Our opinions are just that, and therefore we, as a society, should stop the dissemination and perpetuation of lies. We should be busy enough in our own lives that we do not care about disseminating the stories of others or casting their dirt in the sand. I believe that not only do we almost never know the whole truth, but as human beings, we hear only what we want to hear and see only what supports what we want to hear. We obtain our alleged facts and information through third parties in order to formulate our biasness and speed up our "fact-finding." Anytime we obtain information from others, we must be wary, as it can be riddled with taint, embellishment, falsification, innuendo, rumor, speculation, and the like.

People intentionally spin information in ways that best suits themselves or their stories. I, for instance, have championed the art of disinformation. I intentionally provide people with false information as I am expecting people to use what I tell them against me, and when they do, I can easily prove their stories false.

We continue to pour our subjectivity, feelings, gossip, perceptions, innuendo, speculation, and conjecture into our self-formed fiction, which we later assert as nonfiction. In this game called Life, we must always be wary of those who enjoy a good story and those who seem to enjoy telling them.

If you know someone who lies, someone who preys on others, someone who would pull others down in order for that person to boost his or her own ego, then I want you to run from that person. Even if that person is a friend or a friendly associate, distance yourself. If not, prepare to be eaten. I have learned this fact the hard way.

While there are times when it is good to be around a strong carnivore or predator, understand that you may become the predator's next meal. Utilize the strong for your benefit, if you need protection, but don't turn your back on these predators and don't let them into your life. Remember the story of Little Red Riding Hood. When the Big Bad Wolf got into Grandma's house, all he wanted to do was eat Little Red Riding Hood, and this after already gobbling up Grandma. Greed.

Don't be so naive as to believe you can control predators or carnivores. Use them when you need their force and might. Lose them immediately after. Politely and quickly distance yourself; provide no forwarding contact information.

As if we didn't have enough shit to worry about, we now have to worry about the actions of others. Yes, you do. We have to concern ourselves with the lies, deceit, and trickery of those within the Dark Side. We even must concern ourselves with the collateral damage coming from the rumors, lies, and gossip told by others. Gossip is entrenched within our lives. Entire magazines, TV shows, radio shows, lunch meetings, tea parties, and supermarket shelves are dedicated to the mission of disseminating stories at the expense of others. Gossip is just another name for an intentional spreading of a self-motivated *lie*. As people love a good story, many times this good story will foster and perpetuate itself. It's sad how many people are so miserable that they want to know the gossip and misery of others in order to make themselves feel better.

When opinions are passed off as truth, they do nothing more than cause harm. Game shows, talk shows, tabloids, paparazzi, periodicals, news shows, videos, and other forms of media entertainment thrive on the perpetuated lie being passed off as a truth. People actually pay to hear more of it. The innocent are forced to deal with it. The gossipers get the positive attention they sought. Our own laptop computers twist, pervert, and distort the truth. Photoshop can manipulate any photo, and one might later be used as evidence that you were with someone you shouldn't have been with or somewhere that you weren't. And yes, people will do this in order to profit off of your misery and their trickery. A lie takes on its own form, as people will hear and believe what they want.

Perception comes in all forms. For instance, have you noticed that it is almost always a wrongdoer who would swear he or she was the victim of the situation? As a businessman and a longtime graduate of the University of Hard Knocks, I have been screwed by a lot of people. Believe me that I do not say that proudly, but as I must leave the safety of my home, I become subjected to Life's dangers. The more I put myself out there, the more I subject myself to greater dangers. I will also regrettably tell you that I haven't met a good con artist that I didn't like. That is why con artists are successful, they are so likable.

Everyone will eventually fall prey to someone. It is unavoidable. We live, work, and hide among the many, but eventually, we all fall within the purview of predators. Eventually, even the biggest and strongest wildebeest falls victim to the lion, the lion to the crocodile, the crocodile to the drought, the drought to the new season, and the new season to the hurricane, which of course Life will hit my house right after I just relandscaped my lawn and put on the new roof, which had only a limited warranty.

We must all learn to run, hide, duck, and become invisible in order to survive within this game of Life. Call it hurricane preparation. This is the secret to easy living and keeping your blood pressure under control without the aid of medicine. Life is not easy, and neither is anything we do within Life, so why would you expect anything but difficulties? Do yourself a favor and take great pains to keep chaos out of your living.

Chapter 28

VICTIMS OR EVIL

It is amazing how the same people who have caused you harm are the first to swear that they are the actual victims. I hate these people. These are the people that cannot and do not take responsibility for their own wrongful conduct. These are the people who have messed up or simply didn't do as well as they wanted, so they blame you and me.

Today's society breeds people who blame others for their own misdeeds or misdoings. I have watched these people intentionally hurt others, lie to all, and do what they have to in order to benefit themselves. These people are another type of con artist; only their actions and intentions are more extreme and personal then the average street con artist, who is only trying to make a quick buck and then scram.

Those who need to blame others for their own shortcomings often create cover stories in order to justify their blame game against others. These individuals become the first ones to speak out and make sure everyone who will listen will first get their side of the story, portraying their innocence and explaining why they are now a victim to their own shortcoming. When you point out to them that their arguments are flawed or that you cannot believe the facts as portrayed, these people become agitated, aggressive, ruthless, devious, and simply evil. How dare others doubt or challenge their story?

Life lends itself to people blaming and accusing others for so many reasons. The accusers' motives, as well as those of their witnesses must be scrutinized. Money and opportunity can turn even the holiest of priests into self-motivated liars, connivers, and criminals.

Guard What Is Yours

Never play the middle. Always pick a side. Sooner or later, the party on the right and the party on the left will wind up hating the person who tried to stay in the middle. They will hate you because you didn't pick their side and, therefore, are not their friend. You will be perceived as the friend of the enemy and, thus, the enemy. So much for not wanting to get involved; it sucks, but hey that's Life.

In a business context, such as employer versus employee, if an employee thinks he or she is irreplaceable he or she will seek from the employer much more than a pat on the back. Employees will be the first to rationalize in their own minds that they deserve more. An enterprising employee will believe that he or she is not being rewarded fairly and look how to become their employer's competitor.

In a partnership context, a partner who cannot sufficiently contribute to a partnership should not necessarily become an immediate partner. This person may be a good friend, but do not make such a person your partner until he or she can appropriately contribute. Appropriate contribution must be more than just time and emotional support; your dog can accomplish that. If you want, give the person a partnership option to be used when he or she can contribute appropriately.

Do not allow employees to call themselves your partners when, in fact, they are not. I once allowed an independent contractor, who was a friend, to call himself my partner. I thought, *What can it hurt?* And he was doing fine by the ladies making such representations. The next thing I knew, I was involved in threatened lawsuits, as he was executing contracts on behalf of the company that he was not really a partner in. Lesson learned.

Whenever you engage in business, from the beginning, get a lawyer. I know this is the same as hiring the devil, but it's a necessary evil. Set up employment contracts or memorandums of understanding and understand that you have *no* friends in business. Legally, dot your *i*'s and cross your *t*'s. As the saying goes, "The devil is in the details." If you wait until later to get the details done, it won't happen. Do things correctly from the beginning; the rules of your business and partnership are too important to put off. Spend the money, for if not, it will cost you lots and lots more down the road. When drafting these agreements, do not let the lawyers interfere with the business as you intended. Lawyers will always have suggestions and always look to imbed themselves within the deal or the business or be looking out for more work. Let the lawyers write the legalese, but don't allow them to reshape what you are doing or trying to accomplish.

Today, you are buddies with the person who wants to be your business partner; tomorrow, he'll be ripping you off and trying to sleep with your wife. With technology as it is, keep everyone away from your personal and company e-mails and online information. I have seen many people blackmailed by those with access to passwords and Web site setup information.

Wake up and guard your henhouse. Your henhouse should be defined as your family, business, and home. Your business, spouse, and kids are your hens. Remember that more than one rooster wants the same hen, and if it isn't a rooster, it'll be the cats, dogs, and the butcher. The point is this—your henhouse is always under siege. Life does not allow you to live or work in peace, as there is always more to do and to protect. Keep your guns loaded my friends and keep your mind and eyes sharp.

In protecting your hens, take the position that everybody is a suspect. If you have ever gone through a divorce, you understand that even your spouse can be a double agent and tomorrow's worst nightmare. Life has also demonstrated that your own offspring can sell you out; turn on you; or plan your death out of greed, envy, and dysfunction. Children believe that, because they are yours, your shared blood grants automatic entitlements and succession to your hard work, sacrifices, and all that you have built.

I once had a case in which I was defending a doctor involved in such a tangled web only Life or Disney World could have scripted it. Two doctors had a partnership. I represented the older of the two, who was about sixty-five years old. His partner was significantly younger, about forty-three. My client was married to a luscious, extremely spoiled and unreasonable thirty-five-year-old South Beach hottie. She wanted children. However, I got the feeling that she didn't want to challenge her body. My client already had kids, and didn't want more. While my client had the sexy, young wife, he really didn't. My client no longer wanted to parade around South Beach and shoot shooters at beach bars.

As any good story goes, the younger partner was having an affair with my client's wife. As the story continued, the forty-three-year-old had gotten himself into all kinds of debt and financial trouble while living Life la vida loca on South Beach. His financial concerns had taken a tailspin and debt, beach models, fast toys, and an expensive new waterfront condominium were choking him.

This younger partner, as a means of getting out of debt, embarked on committing Medicare fraud, using my client's name and billing number on the claims. The younger partner set up my client should there ever be a fallout. My client had no idea what was about to run him over and shake up his life forever.

I met my client when he was referred to me after receiving an investigation letter from the Florida Medicare Fraud Task Force. My client sounded completely incensed regarding the letter, and before he came to see me later that week, a law enforcement investigator had already paid him a visit. Shortly thereafter, my client was arrested, still screaming his innocence. In shock and absolute denial, my client would have committed suicide. However, he truly believed that he was just sleeping in a nightmare and would soon wake up. My client had absolutely no idea what he had done, why such horrible things were happening to him, or why such suffering had befallen him and his family. He could not understand the accusations, and the frustrations were agonizing. Yet the evidence, on its face, was convincingly contradictory to my client's proclamations of innocence.

However, something, something just didn't seem right; the evidence against him was too perfect. My client was smart, and such an evidence trail would have been too stupid should he have really been the one committing this type of white-collar crime.

No story would be complete without a wicked witch. My client needed his money to pay the bail and legal expenses. His children were self-sustaining, but he distanced himself from them due to despair and shame. Depression set in, and he couldn't get out of bed. His shock eventually wore off, and he began recognizing his most unfortunate predicament. His lovely wife soon left him and moved close to the partner. Heated legal discovery ensued, and we were able to uncover the story's true plot.

As the storybook was nearing its end, a deal was worked out with the government, to the benefit of my client. My client's partner was arrested. The ex-wife admitted to the affair and testified to various facts, which told of her lover's financial desperation, promises to marry her, desire to get her pregnant, and the conspiracy against his best friend and her then husband.

My client did not go back to jail, but the ordeal left him forever changed. Approximately a year later, I was in a restaurant, Capital Grill, having lunch with some friends. While sitting and talking, I felt someone put her hands around my eyes from behind me and heard a woman's voice ask, "Guess who?"

I took the hands away from my face and turned around; it was my turn to be shocked. Not only was it my client's ex-wife, but she was having lunch with the very same FBI agent who was working the case against her husband! I wish these two the best of luck, as they deserve each other. I hope Life keeps them on the game board for a long, long time.

Chapter 29

TIME AS AN ALLY

My old Sicilian roommate used to always say, "Time tells no lies." The darker the force within a certain person, the quicker his or her true colors will surface. Within a relatively short period of time, you will learn everything you need to know about a person. Characteristics such as malice, a harmful nature, greed, stupidity, jealousy, or envy will quickly surface. When doing business with or beginning a relationship with someone, allow for time, and you'll discover the truth of this person's character.

I am sure that we have all said, "If I had only known . . ." We were not watching for the wolf in sheep's clothing. Wolves must burn a lot of energy in order to hunt. In order to hunt, they must show themselves. All you have to do is wait and watch.

My wife and I purchased a large piece of property. This purchase was not planned. Through another individual, we met a farmer who owned this absolutely lovely parcel of land. We let the farmer slightly into our world, as he would talk and tell his stories.

The first time we went to the property, we actually had a wonderful experience. Phone calls, visits to our home, gifts of wine and cheese, and an interest in our business ensued. He even became a customer in our stores. Two weeks or so later, we were invited for a barbeque on his property and were to bring our children. My wife, being kind, accepted but forgot about the event shortly thereafter. That was no problem because, on the following Thursday, the farmer called with his reminder notice.

Saturday's barbeque was delightful. The property was magnificent and truly unique, with its rainforests, waterfalls, abundant nature, and views. My wife called it "dreamy." During the day, the farmer began telling us how he had tried to develop this property but because of this and that had failed. The excuses were always that he was victimized by people trying to take advantage of him, as he was just a poor farmer. I can relate, being just a dumb cowboy from Chicago.

During the next month or so, this farmer and his daughter made us his new best friend. He was always showing up at one of our stores and making it a point to let us know he and his family had become loyal clients. Ah, I bet you now see where this is going.

One day, the farmer showed up at the house with a bottle of wine and asked to sit with us. We knew he was having financial problems but never gave him a chance to get into it, as we didn't want his issues becoming ours. Sitting on our couch, the farmer immediately began divulging his dire financial condition to us and his need to quickly sell his land. My wife and I weren't sure how to respond, as we were not in the market. His offers continued downward until the price became interesting. A long discussion ensued, and his representations regarding the uses, allowances, and permissions for the property caught our attention. We agreed to some more due diligence trips to the property, where the farmer proudly walked my wife, me, and my wife's parents around the property. We followed up with another trip by four-wheel drive through the property's interior to visit gorgeous, untouched waterfalls and primary rainforest.

The subsequent week, the farmer came to us basically on his knees. He told us that his financial desperation could no longer wait and that, if we were to do this deal, it had to be now. Our lawyer sat with us all and went through a checklist of needs. A fast closing was scheduled, and we laid down our deposit within the following week. The price was almost too good to be true, but one man's loss is another man's gain, right?

Subsequent to the closing, the farmer, now very happy, maintained his friendship. In fact, since my wife and I had lots going on in our lives and the farmer knew the property the best, the farmer insisted that he become very proactive in helping us and our representatives obtain permits for residential development purposes. We wanted immediate actions taken concerning the property, such as securing various permits; obtaining material documents, which the farmer still owed to our lawyer; and permissions to subdivide the land.

The farmer was very helpful and put into place what we assumed were the right people for the jobs at hand. In truth, he put into place the right people to help himself. For instance, we later learned that the topographer he hired was his best friend and was busy redrafting the property borders so that the actual coordinates were smaller than what we'd purchased, whereby adding more land onto the farmer's son's never-before-mentioned existing neighboring lands. This topographer was busy redrafting water coordinates so that varying water sources close to both our boundaries would wind up on his land, whereby depriving our community of natural water sources. This was incredibly stupid, as the farmer had registered with the local and national government the property's borders as well as the water springs, which all had to be concessioned by the national water authority. In order to concession the water springs, they each had to be marked with GPS coordinates and registered within a property map. Oops.

Well, to make a long story short, we asked for a formal meeting, with lawyers present, in order to go over our list of gripes. At that juncture, we didn't want blood. We just wanted a simple solution, such as for the farmer to get the hell away from us and for us not to pay him any more money given the new damages he had caused and cost us.

The meeting took place at our lawyer's office. The farmer showed up with his own entourage. After we'd laid out our case, his lawyers asked for an independent meeting room so that they could talk to their client. Approximately forty minutes later, they all reappeared. We were informed that the farmer had fired his lawyers, as he didn't like being told that he had committed egregious, criminal fraud.

The farmer sought new counsel. Finally, an enterprising lawyer took his case. Our list of frauds and misrepresentations had tallied up to an amazing eighty-five-page brief, not including our supporting documental evidence. The farmer, now caring only about his reputation and pigheaded stubbornness, wanted a trial, as he kept saying we had insulted his good name. His lawyer filed frivolous suits against us and prayed for a settlement. A settlement was not going to happen, and we filed our own slew of lawsuits and damage demands.

A year later, we got our day in court. The farmer lost, of course, but that is not the issue. Life bit us with misery, exhaustion of resources we did not have, mental and emotional torture, loss of sleep, and a strain on our marriage. It even got worse, as my own lawyer began hitting on my wife. He even went as far as insisting that my wife make him her partner in our land. People are absolutely amazing. The only positive was that the farmer's lawyer didn't get paid, and I'm certainly not going to pay mine.

Chapter 30

LIFE'S EVIL TOOLS

A word of advice—do not prejudge other people's successes, as you have no idea what it took that person to get there. Success is individualized and not something that applies evenly. Success can be defined in many aspects and does not have to be material or monetary. Perceived success is as dangerous as guessing whether gossip is true. Perceived financial success can be like an iceberg; you don't know how deep a person's true debts or financial stress go down.

Don't be jealous or envious of other people's green pastures. First, what other people have is not yours. Do not believe you are entitled to what other people have; you are not entitled. Second, you don't know what kind of suffering it took to create such pastures. Third, be happy for others. Fourth, stay this person's friend, as he or she is letting you use his or her pasture; enjoy it. Last, you are only looking at the surface of that pasture and have no idea whether the construction was worth it or the costs were too tolling, what blood lies underneath it, and what its upkeep costs and problems are.

My advice, be happy for others and what they want to promote as their success. It's okay to let others embellish a bit or take pride in what they have. Let them enjoy their pasture and you go enjoy your own or use of theirs. If they are willing to share it, you are the winner. You will get to participate or share in their materiality without having to purchase or maintain it. Being friends with the boat owner is better than owning the actual boat.

Envy Breeds Contempt and Harm

Envy is just as dangerous as greed. People will want your life if they perceive it to be better than theirs. People just want. They justify their desires or actions by claiming to be your victim or rationalizing their due in some illogical way. It is also easier to take than it is to create. My advice again is to remain underneath the radar and out of people's sight. If they don't know you have, then they won't plan on taking.

Judge and live Life not by the size of your wallet, the car you drive, the pointless electronic toys you have or the house you live in. You must create a balance between work, family, enjoyment, entertainment, and your ambitions. I am not saying that you shouldn't shoot for the stars. Go for it. However, I am saying that it is okay if you only get as high as the clouds. It's okay if you undershoot. Maybe it's just not your time to reach the stars. At least you got a good climb and the exercise. Also remember that the stars are not for everybody. Do not feel that you have to reach for the stars if you are happy with the clouds. The clouds are easier to obtain, and once you are there, you can relax, while the overachiever is still trying to climb the stairway to heaven.

For those who do reach the stars, there will be a price. The stars sparkle, but they have a cost. The stars also burn out. During the flight to the stars, a man or woman grows and feels the power of his or her engines. The higher these people soar, the larger their ego, their desires, their lusts, and their cravings for power. Never is a man less loyal and less of a friend than on his rise to the stars. Once there, this man no longer trusts anyone. On top stands a lonely man. Once on top, this man knows that others are on their way up, looking to topple him, as he toppled the last person before him.

Many people just try to reach the stars for materialistic desires. When they crash and burn, they take with them the solar system around them. This collision causes collateral damage, which usually includes you and me. These glory seekers look for rising stars and try to hitch a ride on their comet tails. It is sad that these glory hounds forget about the chances of a crash and burn or, worse, that they will get shot down by another glory seeker on a faster comet.

Opportunities are meant to be seized, but how? Who do you hurt? How badly? Is causing someone else injury so that you can seize the opportunity justified? Is the opportunity yours to make? Is this opportunity something that you have to work for, or is it something that comes too easily? Life has absolutely and unequivocally taught me that nothing should come easy—nothing, and I mean nothing. Life is not easy; nor is anything that you do within it. This means that, if anything comes to you easily, you should forget it. Walk away. In fact, run. No business, no opportunity, no money, no sex, I mean nothing comes easy, unless there will be a hefty price to pay at the end. If something does come easy, then it is probably too good to be true. Gains made from things obtained too easily later get stripped from you with penalties, interests, costs, and fees. Welcome to Life.

Is the Game Too Hard?

Living resembles those crazy video games my children play. The games include lots of violence, fast and fancy hand movements, flashing lights, lots of noise, lack of care or concern, some nudity, and everything that you hope and pray doesn't happen to you. "Doesn't happen to you"—you wish. You cannot shut Life off like you can a video game or TV show. A serious problem we are facing is that every child and some adults have sunk into this virtual reality, where they believe that living has no real consequences. Mimicking TV and games is not reality. My choice for an award-winning reality show is living Life as we know it.

Life's Game Has Swings

What goes up must come down. Let me explain; good people do not sit and plan how to screw other people. Good people do not plot and manipulate situations in order take what is not theirs. Bad people, on the other hand, have this remarkably warped logic that allows them to not only think about doing bad things but to justify their wrongful actions to themselves and their followers. Thus, bad people will do onto others in bad ways, leaving the good people to lose and suffer. While, ultimately, legal actions may prevail for the good people, the bad people enjoy the fruit of their evils for a considerable time, as the wheels of justice turn ever so slowly and expensively. As possession is nine-tenths of the law, the bad usually get away with their wrongful taking and doing.

The stock and real estate markets are good examples of "easy come, easily lost." Many people grew wealthy and greedy in the years between 2004 and August 2008 through the real estate boom. These people placed their own fiscal survival and that of others in jeopardy, all on their own self-assuredness that the markets would continue to rise, they could do no wrong, and they would profit a hero's fortune. Well, guess what? The markets did not continue to rise; hell's gates did open; and these people lost not only their accumulated profits but most, if not all, of their principle. Many of these same people used and lost other investors' hard-earned money or assets in order to account for the principle used. Many of these self-proclaimed geniuses lied, cheated, begged and borrowed, and presented false assurances. Then, when the shit hit the fan, these people screamed the loudest that their losses were and must be the fault of others. These losses certainly could not be their own doing! When you need to blame someone, if not yourself, do what I do; blame my buddy, Matt. Go ahead. Wipe your feet on him.

The investors who blindly followed those they invested in lost, and whether they want to believe it or not, they took and accepted the associated risks. We are all big boys and girls, and when playing with opportunities, we should open our eyes, ask questions, and get answers. We must play responsibly, follow through, and understand our investments. And if the investment works, fantastic. If it doesn't work, which is the more likely scenario, share in some of the blame or don't blame at all. Playing ostrich and burying your head in ignorance does not buy you absolution.

It is impossible to live your life guiltlessly and without skeletons. Everyone who steps into the real world gets battle scars. Everyone has either been shat on or has done the shitting. Sooner or later, the ass that you kicked will wind up being the ass that you have to kiss. The game board is circular, so that everything comes back around and is never ending. Life has ironies and faults, and so do the actions, omissions, and reactions that follow. You must accept certain faults or the fact that "shit happens." Rarely can Life be one-sided. Legal systems do not work to bring justice; nor do they protect the innocent; only I do. (See www. TheBrandLawFirm.com.)

Living requires extensive trials and tribulations, amounting to enormous hardships. Nothing about these hardships and incurred losses are fair, just, or right. I'm sorry for your losses, hurt, and grieving; I share your pain.

Success?

Ask yourself why it is that, every time you climb that corporate ladder, there is someone pulling you down. Only Mom is happy for your success. Well, Eminem's mother isn't, but my mom at least is. People are jealous of your successes and want them. Next time you bring good news to your friends, watch the crookedness of their smiles, as they are thinking just how they can take some of your joy for themselves. When you tell your work associates that you just obtained a bonus or promotion, listen to the post-conversations behind your back. "Why did he get it and not me?" "I deserve it more than he does." "I'm going to talk to the boss and tell him that it is not fair." "Good, now that he got that, how am I going to benefit?"

You won't hear too many comments like, "I'm so happy for him." "He deserves it." "He is a great employee." You won't hear these types of responses because people won't make them unless they can benefit off of you in some way. People simply just have this need to be negative and wish negativity upon others.

My advice, be happy for others when good things are bestowed upon them. Keep positive, stay your course, and your turn will come. Do not take what is not yours and keep your hands and concern in your own pockets, not those of others.

Chapter 31

CAN YOU BE CONTENT WITH WHAT YOU HAVE

There is no end to nice. What I mean by this is that you should be happy with what you have, if what you have is yours. There will always be someone prettier, more handsome, wealthier, smarter, or stronger, and the list goes on and on—in other words, "greener grass." Life will have you pay a huge price for taking another's grass field. The price to pay may not be worth the victory. Furthermore, Life will laugh last when, after you conquer this new, greener grass, it turns brown and withers, as it was not meant for you.

How many times have you heard stories of a husband leaving his wife for a younger woman? Later we learn that the younger woman leaves the older husband for a younger man and takes most of the husband's money in the divorce to enjoy with the younger man. However, this woman will also get her turn, as she will grow older and that younger man will look for a new, younger lady. The Game of Life is a great big, vicious circle.

You must learn to be happy with what you have and stop looking at other people's pastures for conquests. Besides, even if you were able to plant your feet on someone else's pasture, who is to say that this pasture would accept you or be all that you thought it would? If what you have is not broken, do not look to change it. In fact, if it isn't broken, don't window-shop. Don't dream of change, and don't give in to temptation, as temptation will only lead you to trouble. Trouble is simply too easy to encounter, and you will need no help in the finding. If you are looking for conquests, go burn these desires off in the gym. Don't you have enough troubles already?

Learn to simply be happy with what you have and quash your thirst for more and your unchecked ambitions. If you are happy with what you have, with what you are doing, with whom you are with, then stop looking for ways to self-destruct and destroy what you just admitted was a good thing.

Living under the Radar

Learn to live simple or invisible. Do not let people see what it is that is making you happy. To do so only invites envious people into your life in order for them to try to take your happiness. If others don't know what you have, then they won't try to take it, and the happiness will, hopefully, stay with you.

It is so important to live below your means. Learn to be modest and humble and live accordingly. Life cannot shake you so violently when you are on middle ground and have resources. If hidden, these assets will prove most useful and powerful. In fact, you will watch as all of those "flash and cash" friends fall by the wayside and all of the others, who bragged about their wealth, lose it. The laws of physics apply to everything, including Life. What goes up must come down. Life is a pendulum swinging from side to side, extreme to extreme. Today is good, tomorrow is bad, and such is Life.

Another benefit of living low is that people stop asking you for things, favors, or money. I learned to cry poor, and not only did all of the leeches in my life go away, I was no longer put in uncomfortable positions of telling people no. Didn't work on my daughter!

Unchecked Ambitions

Predators never rest. A predator's life is aggressive, and his or her style isn't apt to make friends. Predators are assured a life of aggression, loneliness, and conflict, and their enemies are willing to return the favor.

I once watched an Animal Planet show that depicted the interaction between wildebeests and the predators of the African plains. When wildebeests find the opportunity to trample on or crush predators' cubs, including those of hyenas and lions, they commit this murder with joy in their hearts, as they know those predator cubs will never have the chance of eating one of their own young. This really amazed me, as it proved the theory that everyone, including "the food," comes to a point at which they harbor resentment, hatred, and retaliatory thinking against those who have caused them so much harm. Revenge really is a dish everyone enjoys.

Chapter 32

IS THE PRIZE WORTH THE COST?

S hould you ever get the opportunity to see one, a white elephant is truly a unique animal. While having a white elephant may sound remarkable, impressive, and amazing, you cannot play with a white elephant; it has no loyalty to you; it can be dangerous; you cannot gain "good loving" from it, and the expense of maintaining, securing, and protecting it is ungodly. All in all, you acquired the white elephant out of greed, ego, and ambition. But in the end, it certainly wasn't worth the troubles, concerns, resources, and expenditures, and if you could get rid of it, you would. Also remember that people usually purchase *flash* because they need to show off in order to feel important and calm insecurities. If you are already happy, busy, and content, then you don't need to waste your money on stupidity or show off material possessions. You will only live to secretly wish such expenses and troubles were gone.

Never count someone else's money. Other people's money is not your concern or your business. You cannot count other people's money anyway; nor can you know whether their source of *flash* is backed by real cash, a mortgage, a lease, a loan, or stolen. You may be surprised to learn that someone's *bling* really doesn't belong to them or isn't legitimate. In the end, other people's wealth or lack thereof is irrelevant, as it's still not yours, and they aren't giving it to you. You want such bling, go earn it and be proud of your accomplishments.

Failing is never failing, as you are learning. Think of it more as practice. Learn to fish, and you will never go hungry. Learn only how to eat fish, and you will always be reliant upon others for your food. Learn only how to steal fish, and you will always be a thief and probably a hungry thief.

Live within limits. Live to save, live to be honest, live to work hard, and live to take nothing from others, as others will only want back from you in return and then some. Furthermore, if you take from others, you may become responsible for what you took, and that can be trouble enough. If you want more from Life, then learn to share. By sharing, you can enjoy the benefits of having it all without having to purchase or be responsible for everything. Sharing is a difficult human concept, as it means playing nicely with others, having joint respect, and treating other people and their belongings with tender love and care. Once you get the hang of sharing, there is nothing better.

Having Difficulty?

True friendships are few and far between. Ask yourself just how many "best friends" you have had so far in your life? If they were really best friends, then you wouldn't keep changing them! Friends change as your Life changes. Family and true friends should be there for you, regardless, not add to your existing headaches.

It is dangerous to trust others with your secrets and personal information, even your best friend. Not even your priest should know your troubles or passwords. Have them, hide them, never share, and if you have to talk about them, talk in riddles and false stories.

Remember that people love gossip and revealing secrets. People use other people's weaknesses against them. Today's friends are tomorrow's enemies. Information is power. Please, please, please, learn to shut your mouth and don't allow anyone other than, maybe, Mommy to know your secrets or weaknesses. I promise you that friendships are short, and most friends become *rats*. Mommy would most likely be willing to protect you. If you have a need to talk, I would recommend going back to sleep. If you are not tired, then either talk to your dog, talk to yourself, or go for a long walk.

Our current generation of children does not understand the meaning of loyalty and trust. Today's generation only knows of such concepts through movies and TV shows such as *The Godfather* and *The Sopranos*, but watching the screen is different than learning honor from the streets. There were once days in which loyalty and trust was a man or woman's bond. The sacredness of honor amongst thieves was a religion, not a phrase. If what information a friend or family learned of was through trust then it must be safeguarded no matter what and in spite of your relations tomorrow. Today's generations are more inclined to tattletale or snitch than be honor bound.

Travel Light and Stay Thirsty, My Fellow Travelers

Evil has learned to shape-shift; don't get caught off guard. We walk around oblivious to the dangers that Life has in store. We act more like wildebeests at the river's edge than wise owls or learned monkeys. Recognize a crocodile and its camouflage. Recognize that danger is always lurking. Never believe you are bulletproof. It is better to back away from waters you are not certain about then to put your foot into the crocodile's mouth.

Life is easier with less. Survival requires you to travel fast and light. Travel with what you truly need and recognize that anything else is a luxury.

People's jealousy will play a role in their desire to have or their secondary hatred toward you for having what they don't. Their envy will cause them to prey upon your source of happiness, and this is where Life and its Dark Side really have fun.

"Life Sucks" Is Synonymous to "No Shit, Sherlock"

Look at your smile. How much do you smile? Do you smile? How long does your smile last? I bet not long enough. I am sure that you spend your days yearning for something more, something for you, some sort of constant happiness—something that makes you want to live. Then hide that happiness before Life strips it from you.

We have lost control of our lives. Our destiny is caught up in so many twists and turns. Our heads are exploding, our troubles are mounting, and our souls are drowning. The systems we work and live are all broken. The lines between right and wrong have been crossed so many times that morality has taken on a new definition.

Right, wrong, yes, no, questions, and answers are all blurry. Laws no longer provide justice. We are an opinionated culture. We formulate beliefs and call them facts when they are based upon only our own arrogance or ignorant innuendo. We prejudge and create conclusions based upon other third-party recitations of only the parties' perceived beliefs. We are wrong, indifferent, callous, and disheartened. We only think we are right, great, loved, and above all else. We love the tabloids because reading about other people's problems makes us feel better.

As a successful trial lawyer, I was miserable. My family gave way to career. I always had to stay two steps ahead of my competition for fear that the lawyer next door would be stealing away my clients. I always had to seek new clients. I had no control of my busy schedule, as I always had to run to court, to depositions, to a client's office; I ran here, there, and everywhere. My office, in reality, was my prison. My life was not mine but belonged to everyone else. At the end of the day, I was so tired from fighting for my clients' rights that I couldn't fight for my own. At midnight, still at my desk with a pile of documents and a late-night Burger King snack, I quickly learned the value of whiskey. God bless alcohol. The fancy cars, nice house, boat, helicopters, and private planes were becoming less and less important. In fact, I cursed myself for getting these fancy toys in the first place. These toys were my pity vice and were, for me, a momentary sense of purchased happiness. They were my white elephants. Now, as I reminisce, I only wish I could have the money I spent back.

Life doesn't give a shit about your remorse. I had to go through all of the above vices in order to try to find some happiness. I learned that the grass isn't greener elsewhere. I also learned that money does not buy you lasting happiness. Money buys you that momentary smile, but that is all it buys you.

It is important that people learn to open their arms and flap their wings if they are to fly. If you do not learn to fly and take chances, then you will go nowhere and have no vision to better yourself. Change is a positive aspect of Life. Change is frightening. If you are using change as a way to improve Life, then by all means, flap those arms. If you fall, try again and again. Practice over water! Eventually, you will fly or find a way to accomplish the same through creativity. If you don't try, if you give up, if you quit, if you lack the courage or persistence, you will never accomplish what your ambitions and goals were meant to achieve. Never be afraid to ask, seek, and ask again. If you don't ask, you will certainly not get what you want. If you don't try, it is certain that you won't achieve.

People get so caught up in their forced reality that they wind up no longer knowing what happiness is. A fun Saturday night is *not* happiness; it is a moment. Life allows you to enjoy a night in order to keep you fit for the hell that is to come tomorrow. Look around. What do we do all day, each day? We fight, we worry, we stress about our problems and conflicts. We need lawyers, professionals, advisors, doctors, plumbers, and electricians. In today's society, everything is a lawsuit, everything is a law, and everything is a stifling. We have constant worries and concerns. We have health problems, family issues, headaches, childhood associated traumas, adulthood traumas, financial worries, and job concerns. And some of you might be thinking, *Job, what job? I wish.* We bust our asses and get nowhere. We can't seem to pull ahead, or if we do, it too is short-lived. We have children and then suffer their problems. This is the summation of life. This sucks.

My mom would beg to differ, but I know she too is only fooling herself or simply saying that Life's grand in order to try to comfort both her and her family. Or maybe I'm correct; she is delusional.

In reality, you should recognize that Life is nothing more than problems and attempts at solving them. Nothing can be preplanned, as nothing will go as planned. Adapt in order to survive. Life has caused us to create difficulties and complexities of such grand proportions that we are no longer capable of handling them.

Overprotecting our children, more often than not, only provides them with short-term comfort. A child must grow up understanding that Life isn't all pink and roses. A child must understand that Life is difficult and unfair. Mom must not completely shield her family from

Life's sadness but explain to them that this is how Life is and that they must grow strong and hard to its difficulties and cruelties. In fact, children must be shown to expect the unexpected no matter how ugly. If not, children will not know how to handle the stress in their lives, now and in the future. Children must learn about stress and how to cope and resolve stress by experiences. It is only through experiences that one learns what to expect in the future and how to solve the issue the next time.

Children, do not allow your stresses to turn into anxieties. What you are experiencing is what we all experience or have experienced and gotten through. If I can work through my stresses, then so can you. You are better than I am. Break down the situation into manageable components, breathe, and think about what is happening and what you must do in order to get through the situation. Stress will cause your brain to think faster. Just don't compound the error. Don't stop to cry, don't panic, and don't allow Life to break you. You are smart; you will persevere. When overstressed or burdened, stop before panic or anxiety sets in; rationalize where it is you must go, be at, or do in order to come out of the experience safe. Cry afterward; but I promise you that your tears will be from accomplishment not from being grief stricken.

Chapter 33

GROWING UP

We grow up unchallenged and without sufficient knowledge of the real world and how we must be prepared for the sorrows that are sure to come. Our children expect Mercedes Benzes, which we have allowed to not only warp their sense of reality but puts unfair pressures upon us, as we try to please or impress them on a Chevy budget. We must stop this nonsense. Kids must conform to reality just as we must. There is nothing wrong with you or your parenting if you can't purchase a Mercedes. You should explain to your children why you are not purchasing a Mercedes and make the explanation an education. If your children still do not understand, check their diets for lead paint.

Mom should educate children on just how much money Life costs. During this educational session, Mom can show the kids the need to save and to think twice about the necessity of the item in question. Remember, a penny saved is a penny earned.

By far the most important Life lesson is to learn how to do things for yourself and, if you fail, learn how to have the courage to try again and again and, if need be, again. Mothers need to push their children to become independent and helpful. Children, as well as you, must be independent, knowledgeable and know how to do for themselves without being told to do so. We must teach our children the basic skills to fend for themselves, to take basic care of themselves, to defend themselves, and to survive. Spoiled children will have the hardest time facing and rationalizing Life's disappointments and hardships.

Youth is wasted on the young. By the time you understand this phrase, you are already too old to enjoy living in the manner you once dreamed about. When you think it is your time to finally enjoy those golden years, *wham*, you're hit with your first heart attack, cancer, diabetes, high blood pressure, high cholesterol, or whatever other ailment might befall you. Instead of champagne and caviar, it is now IV fluids and hospital bills. When I was young, all I wanted was a fire-engine red Porsche. Now I'm too old and fat to enjoy it. Life sucks.

The Lessons of Barney, Mr. Rogers, and Bill Cosby

I am here to tell you that buying happiness is very short term and, in the end, only adds to unhappiness. Perhaps an example will help exemplify my point: You buy the fancy, new car. Now you must worry about it—you worry about damage, theft, how much it constantly sets you back, and speeding tickets. The examples are endless and can be applied everywhere and to almost everything. I once heard a joke on point; "If it flies, floats, or fucks, lease it!"

We have been duped into believing that Life is a wonderful event, a meaningful event, an event that can be destined and controlled and is ours for the taking. Ladies and gentlemen, Life is not ours to control or take. Life is not about fairness, bad or good luck, or questions of what you might have done in the past or why you find yourself in certain positions. Life contains more bad, evil, and unfairness than it does goodness and justice, so accept this and face reality.

Life has further separated us from what I call "the Cosby Lessons" or "Barney and the Gang." Both Bill Cosby and Barney—yes, the big, purple dinosaur—try to teach our children that we don't have to use foul language but should use manners, courtesy, respect, and politeness. As these guys would have it, "Please and thank you are the magic words," and, "sharing is caring."

Sharing should be an automatic learned concept. It is a wonderful concept, as it teaches us how to better interact with each other, how to make friends, and how to play nicely together. The concept of lending to each other is very much like how partnerships and relationships work. Wow! These actions and interactions are skills needed in the real world. Unless you want your children to grow up as lone wolves, they must know how to share and play nicely with others. Kids, are you listening?

Part of sharing and playing with others is knowing how to lose. Be graceful when you lose. Competitiveness is fine as long as lines are not crossed. If you do lose, understand that this is part of Life. Even lions come back from the hunt with more losses than kills. An unsuccessful hunt is practice for tomorrow's kill. Thus, losing does not make you a "loser"; it makes you seasoned for tomorrow.

Chapter 34

GETTING TO
THE CONCLUSION

What's life without a few bumps? What's life without its ups or downs? Life equals problems, the problems are *big*, and society is drowning. Relationships are drowning. Despair and desperation are all that most of us are left with. I am asked if I am depressed. I just don't know any more, as I can no longer gauge what normal is. I believe that Life has beaten the majority of us up so badly that, should there be anyone who considers him or herself "normal," this is the person who needs a psychologist. This would be the person who is different. We all handle posttraumatic stress disorder differently, and there is no way that any of us walk away from Life's mistreatments without receiving some sort of unbalance. Stay thirsty, my friends, and drink heavily.

I saw a new medicine that some genius thought of and marketed. This pill is for those who have money problems, life troubles, family woes, children problems, spousal issues, or stress concerns or those whose job sucks. In other words, this pill is for all of us. You will be able to purchase this pill at select pharmacies. Ask for one thousand milligrams of Fukitol.

If you don't like my theory that hell is really for the living, then let's flip the theory and see if you like an alternate theory. Follow this twist; maybe we are dead but just don't realize it yet. We are in hell, living hell. Think about it. You are wondering why Life sucks, why such bad things are happening and happening to you, why nothing seems to go well. After all, Mommy said that Life was roses, and this Life is no bed of roses.

If I'm in a living hell, then I'm actually okay with Life! I'm enduring no fire and brimstone or peeling off of my skin. Hell sucks, but now that I know where I am and why Life is treating me like this, I can understand, accept, and deal with it. I even got to keep my lawyer's bar card which makes me an officer down here.

Do you think it is a coincidence that the cosmetic companies are pushing all of these antiaging solutions upon us? No; they have seen society age and want to offer us hope and a prayer. Like slapping on some night cream will really bring the fountain of youth. If I had to rub on a certain percentage of cream commensurate with my stress levels and premature aging, I would have to bathe in it instead.

If you allow hatred and contempt to fill your soul, it will. A person looking for trouble will find it. Negative vibrations will cause good people to run from you. Negativity will only attract negativity. Positivity creates more opportunity. Move forward with your life and leave the past where it belongs—in the past.

I believe Walt Disney World to be our savoir. Imagine that. Life sucks so badly that we must look to a hundred-year-old mouse for a week's worth of smiles. The problem is, when you get your credit card bill and see just how much that mouse cost, your smile will disappear. Now factor in the price of gas!

It appears that Life's lessons are never finished. I have learned that, even when I am right, I am wrong. If I stand up for myself, I am the asshole; if I don't stand up for myself, then I'm either a wimp or guilty. Does that happen to you as well? If I'm frustrated or yell, then I'm the bad guy. If I'm nice, then I get taken advantage of. If I voice my opinion or want to be noticed, I am being difficult. If I raise my voice in disagreement, people get upset with my dissent. We just can't win for trying, can we?

Life can be cruel in other ways. Take, for instance, the good father who has spent his life making his family happy and simply struggling to do his best to hold it all together. His youngest child is now through school, just married, and has taken a good job. It is now Dad's turn to finally enjoy his golden years. Not feeling well, he goes to the doctor and is told mortal news. The golden years for which he has been waiting his whole life now turn shit brown. Life sucks. Thus, Dad, spend it now, while you can enjoy it. Party on and save some for Mom.

This morning, my wife and I awoke happy. My wife had to be at a municipal meeting concerning a residential development that we were building, and I had to actually be at the development site. Since the municipality was on the way to the project, I followed my wife. My wife's meeting was scheduled for 8:00 a.m. and was an hour away. Arriving at the municipality a little early, my wife received a phone call saying that the meeting had been changed to 9:00 a.m.; "Sorry." This means I had to wait another hour before getting to the job site and my morning coffee.

At 9:20 a.m., my wife was finally shown into the municipal conference room. I waited with her until her meeting began and then headed to the project, another fifteen minutes later.

Our project is up on a mountain with one road up and down. At points, the road gets very steep. As I was heading up the road, I got caught behind several large dump trucks, hauling gravel and road rock to the project. Being Costa Rica, it was, of course, raining and hard. For those of you who have never been to the rainforest during rainy season, I want you to imagine rain the size of hail and hail the size of meteorites. Anyway, these fully loaded dump trucks were having a rough time with the incline, the hard rains, the muddy conditions, and a slippery road. These trucks were forcing me to put my own car through hell. I had to go constantly in and out of first gear and many times into an emergency reverse as the dump truck in front of me would suddenly begin sliding backward. My Land Rover was not very happy, and at one point, I had to stop, get out of the car in the rain, and cry as one of those fucking dump trucks had just sprayed thirty-five feet of heavy gravel all over the front of my car, destroying my beautiful paint. These dump trucks created mud trenches. Given my slow speed, I began sliding downward; now my transmission was not having fun. The rains were so hard, that not only was my vision gone, but also the rains filled the trenches, causing me to drive my poor car by brail.

I hit one of these trenches hard and heard a huge explosion. Wonderful. The explosion was so loud that the dump truck ahead of me stopped in a panic, as he thought he'd dropped his gravel load. Nope; it was my SUV. It was pouring rain, and I was still approximately a quarter of a mile or so from the project's office. The driver of the truck in front of me continued up the mountain and sent help.

My beautiful wife was having her own headaches. Her meeting was supposed to be simple and pretty much routine. We had submitted plot maps, which were overdue, to be rubber-stamped by the muni. By law, the municipality only has ten days to reject any submitted lot plans, and if it intended to deny the plans, the municipality had to set forth the specific reasons; otherwise, the plans would be granted as a matter of law. The municipality did not reject our plans, and the ten days had lapsed. Nothing was wrong with these plans; they mirrored already approved plans. The meeting finally started, and my wife was told that the municipality would not be stamping these individual lot plans because (now dig this) the previous owner of the property who'd sold it to us years ago was suing the municipality for who knows what, and they were upset with him.

There is an adage that states, "A friend of an enemy is an enemy." The municipality assumed that we were friends with the farmer who sold us the land, and, thus, now we too were the municipality's enemy. The resulting logic was that the municipality now was not going to do anything that would help us. Talk about a stunning abuse of power. Welcome to the jungle.

In hindsight, it was a good thing that I was experiencing certain car troubles, as I might have driven my Land Rover right through the municipality conference room upon hearing this news. I would have gone down as one of those disgruntled postal shooters!

It took two weeks to get my Land Rover back from the shop. Poor car, it suffered block problems and a blown muffler, and three of the four engine mounts broke. I am amazed that the CD player never skipped a beat! During these two weeks, we had to sit with, meet, and plead our case before the mayor, the city commission, and a roomful of high-priced lawyers. The stress was enormous, the costs extremely high, and our project in complete limbo, as we couldn't do anything with a hostile municipality. After two weeks of meetings, crying, and pleading, the municipality finally released its stranglehold on us. My lawyers say it was due to their great efforts and threats of suits. Bullshit; it was the municipal board finally realizing that I was about to kill this farmer myself, and they didn't want the liability. The board members realized that an enemy of an enemy is a friend, and we shared a common enemy.

CONCLUSION

L ife isn't even kind enough to leave us alone when we finally survive to our supposed golden years. These golden years should be a gift, a pleasure, and a blessing—*peace*. No, Life has seen fit to make our golden years the hardest survival test yet. Haven't we gone through enough bullshit? Now you are telling me that getting older really means living will be getting harder. Yes, I am.

Getting older means we get to look forward to failing health; an inability to take care of ourselves or our loved ones; pissing and pooping on ourselves; eating through a straw; being disrespected by the community because we are now senior and weak, looked down upon by the youth, and targets for the street scum to rob or maim; money problems that we can no longer solve; lack of employment possibilities; adult diapers; old age facilities; body odor; failed memory; unwanted hair; and the list goes on and on. Only Walt Disney and other sadistic, fortunate few would want to place themselves in cryogenics and live to all eternity. Not me; cut that birthday cake now, as my friends have better things to do than watch me age.

Learn to tell those dear to you that you love them and more often. It is okay to let your feelings show and to express them. You will regret not doing so. Why is it that people only listen to you after you are dead?

Remember that Life takes from you. Life takes from you what you love and need the most. Never count on there being a tomorrow for whatever the reason; but the problem is that we must plan on tomorrow coming and the next tomorrow.

Mom, I love you and thank you for being part of my life and everything else you have done for me, which is enough to be its own book. And, if I don't tell you enough, I love you, Mom, and see, I didn't write an evil book about you after all!

Good luck to you all, and may the Force be with you. I'm going for a beer.